HIDDEN HISTORY *of* WACO

Eric S. Ames

Published by The History Press
Charleston, SC
www.historypress.com

First published 2020

Manufactured in the United States

ISBN 9781467140874

Library of Congress Control Number: 2020932164

Notice: The information in this book is true and complete to the best of our knowledge. It is offered without guarantee on the part of the author or The History Press. The author and The History Press disclaim all liability in connection with the use of this book.

This volume is dedicated to my family: my wife, Amy; and my daughters, Sophia and Audrey; my parents, Patrick (1953–2012) and Marsha; and my brother, Cory, and his wife, Kristyn, for their unwavering support of my authorial pursuits. And, as always, to the fine people of the city of Waco, my adopted hometown and possessor of one of the greatest sets of stories ever told—documented, hidden and yet to be written.

Contents

Contents

Acknowledgements

If you had told me in 2008 that by the year 2020 I would be a thrice-published author, I would have thought you an insane person. If you'd further added that all three of those books would be on the history of Waco—a subject that I have truly learned to love in my fifteen years of living here—I would have told you it was impossible. But this is indeed my third volume, and I am blessed to be given the opportunity once again to shine a light on the history of a place I hold so dear.

This book could not have happened without the previous efforts of a host of Wacoans past: Roger Conger, the former mayor and widely acknowledged Keeper of Waco's Early Memory; the fine people at the Historic Waco Foundation (HWF), whose *Waco Heritage & History* publication is a treasure-trove of city lore; and the newspaper reporters, editors and advertisers whose work fed titles like the *Artesia*, the *Waco Daily News* and the *Waco Daily Advance*. Likewise, the efforts of institutions like the Lockwood Library and Museum, The Texas Collection, the Baylor Libraries' Digital Preservation Services team and the City of Waco all do their part daily to preserve our city's heritage.

I am especially thankful to Sam Moody of the Lockwood Library and Museum, Darryl Stuhr and his team at the DPS, Bill Foster, Jill Barrow of HWF, J.B. Smith of the *Waco Tribune-Herald* and Stephen Sloan of the Institute for Oral History for their support (knowing or unknowing) of this endeavor. I am forever in your debt.

Introduction

Setting out to write a book on the hidden history of a city like Waco is no small task. In fact, one could argue that the history of a place is never actually hidden, as someone at some time was party to the information contained in this volume; much of it has been documented to a greater or lesser extent elsewhere, and some of it may have been carefully secreted away so as to make for a tidier explanation of the city's past. But given the explosion of national interest in Waco that was engendered by the coming of HGTV's *Fixer Upper*, hosted by the city's best-known twenty-first-century ambassadors, Chip and Joanna Gaines, there is a new opportunity to catalogue, explore and promote a fuller understanding of Waco's history to a national audience. That is what this volume seeks to do.

That is not to say that what is contained in these pages is an exhaustive list of Waco's past. An undertaking like that would take volumes and many skilled hands working for years. There are aspects of Waco's history that deserve much more space than I can give them here, particularly the history of African American, Latino, Jewish and other ethnic and cultural minority groups. And while I attempt to bring their voices into the conversation contained in this book, it is beyond my knowledge—and, frankly, my mandate for this work—to tell those stories in the manner in which they deserve to be told.

Likewise, this book will not dive into the histories of some of our more famous people, places and things: the ALICO building, Dr Pepper, Baylor University, the Waco Tornado, the Branch Davidians. All of them are important to Waco's history, and all have been explored in other settings in ways that give them their due respect.

With this book, what I hope to bring to the discussion of Waco's past is an exploration of the stories that haven't received widespread attention in the past ten years, if ever—the stories that explain the names of local landmarks, or the wording on a headstone, or the reason why some names are still whispered in hushed tones around town, if they're even mentioned at all. Some of the stories will be uplifting, others merely interesting, and a few will challenge readers to accept the difficult truth of documenting history. For the truth is that there are events in any town's history that bring with them difficult questions not only about what happened then, but also what we can do to address them now. Some of those stories are documented here, such as the trial and execution of Roy Mitchell or the role of the Ku Klux Klan in 1920s Waco.

Since its establishment in 1849, Waco has grown from a frontier town on the Brazos River to a thriving city of more than 125,000 residents living within its limits. And in those 171 years, the city's citizens have seen triumph, tragedy, humor, heartbreak and infamy. This volume is intended as a thank-you to all Wacoans, past, present and future, who love its stories as much as I do.

I

Reconstruction and the Gilded Age

1

Reflections of "Days Agone" by a Waco Lawyer circa 1876

There are many ways a book on Waco's hidden history could be organized, but the most logical and sensible is to dive back as far into the archival record as is possible and work our way closer to the present. With that in mind, we begin our journey into Waco's lesser-known tales with an examination of a document that was reproduced in the Winter 1974 issue of the Historic Waco Foundation's *Waco Heritage & History*. Titled "Historical Sketch of Waco" and written by Waco attorney Marcus Herring in 1876, the piece offers a Reconstruction-era take on the early years of Waco and McLennan County and paints a picture of what a prominent citizen might have felt about the city's past, present and future.

Herring begins his recollections with excerpts from a speech given by Sam Houston "from a goods box in front of the courthouse to a large assembly of belligerent secessionists." This was in the period right before the start of the Civil War, when Texans were arguing about whether to hold a secession convention. Houston predicted that, should the state vote for secession and a war break out, anyone returning to Waco following the war's end—which would naturally be won by the "national" (Union) side—would find "your business gone, the noxious weeds growing on your streets, and all over this public square business houses unoccupied or bringing in no rent, your families in a state of want and destitution." Further, Houston warned, "As sure as the day follows the night, the course you are taking [supporting secession] will accomplish the very object you wish to prevent: the freedom of your slaves."

WACO DAILY ADVANCE.

VOL. 2. No. 127 WACO, TEXAS, THURSDAY, MAY 29, 1873. SINGLE COPIES, 10 CENTS.

THE WACO ADVANCE (WEEKLY EDITION) Is issued every Thursday Morning, and contains The Latest Telegrams, Latest Market Reports, Foreign and Domestic News, Choice Miscellany, and a general variety of Southern, State and Local News Items.

OUR DAILY Is issued every Morning but Monday, containing Latest Telegrams, News by Mail, Locals and Markets. Single copies, 10c., or 75c. per month. One Year, $8 00

Advertisements inserted at living rates. Transient advertisements payable in advance. Yearly advertisements payable quarterly in advance.

GOLLEDGE & TOMLINSON, Proprietors and Publishers. Office up stairs, cor. Austin Avenue and Fourth street.

Our Authorized Agents.

STRANGERS' GUIDE.

THE ORDERS.

Arrival and Departure of Mails at Waco, Texas.

PROFESSIONAL.

DR. J. C. J. KING, Offers his Professional Services to the citizens of Waco and vicinity. Office up stairs at the Drug Store of Eastland & Co. Residence, corner of 1st and Clay streets.

DR. S. K. SMITH, DENTIST. Waco, Texas. Has fitted up rooms for a permanent stay, and guarantees satisfaction in all lines of work. Teeth extracted without pain, by the inhaling process. Give him a call.

R. W. PARK, M. D., Physician and Surgeon. Office—Eastland & Co.'s drug store, east side public square.

WEST & PRATHER, Attorneys-at-Law, Waco, Texas. Office in Sturgis' building.

DRS. WHITE & BROWN, Physicians and Surgeons, Waco, Texas. Office in the Lusk building, over J. D. Wallace's store. Dr. White may be found at night at the McClelland Hotel. Dr. Brown's residence is on Third street.

J. W. OLIVER, ATTORNEY AT LAW, Waco, Texas. Office on Austin street, over the store of Lyons, Lindenthall & Co.

FORT & JACKSON, BANKERS And Dealers in Domestic and Foreign Exchange. Waco, Texas.

J. E. SEARS, Wholesale and Retail DRUGGIST, WACO, TEXAS. Offers the largest stock of FRESH DRUGS, MEDICINES, PAINTS, OILS, LIQUORS, TOBACCO, And a General Variety of Goods, at LOWER PRICES than was ever offered in this market. JOBBING ORDERS SOLICITED.

E. H. CARTER & CO., Dealers in HARDWARE, Pistols, Axes, Hoes, Horse Shoes, Nails, Carpenters' and Blacksmiths' Tools, Iron Axles, Iron, Steel, Bolts, Chains, Table and Pocket Cutlery, Castings, Boxing, &c., STAPLE DRY GOODS, BOOTS, SHOES, HATS AND NOTIONS. Waco, Texas.

GET YOUR BEEF At the City Market. Having purchased the interest of Tom Richey, in the Richey & Reed market, we are now prepared to fill all orders for Beef, Mutton, Pork, Etc., at any time, and on reasonable terms. REED & BOYD.

FLINT & CHAMBERLIN, BANKERS.

FLINT, CHAMBERLIN & GRAHAM Attorneys and Counselors at Law, Waco, Texas.

FOR SALE AT AUCTION. A Beautiful Residence. WINN, WALLACE & CO., Auctioneers.

COMPARE OUR PRICES WITH OTHERS. THE OLD AND RELIABLE JEWELERS. PRINCE & GOLDSMITH WACO, TEXAS, SELL AMERICAN WATCHES!

In Two-ounce Silver Cases, for	$14 50
In Three-ounce " "	16 25
In Four-ounce " "	18 00
In Six-ounce " "	24 50

And finer grades as cheap in proportion. Solid 18 karat Gents' Gold Watches from $60 to $250; Ladies' $30 to 125.

FOURTEEN KARAT GOLD CHAINS, (The best Manufactured for Durability.) For Ladies, at $18 to $65 00; For Gents, at $13 to $85 00.

EIGHTEEN KARAT PLAIN GOLD RINGS, Weighing two dollars in gold, at $1 90; Three $2 80; Four $3 70; Five $4 60. And so on, and warranted full 18 karat, or no sale.

SPECTACLES, OF ALL GRADES, FROM 25c. TO $12 00.

GOLD THIMBLES, $4 50. SILVER COIN THIMBLES, 35c. TREBLE PLATED AND SILVER WARE, OF ALL KINDS, At invoice cost, and a very large discount given.

Eight Day Clocks, From $4 to $8 50. ONE DAY CLOCKS, from $1 80 to $4.

In fact all articles are sold at greatly reduced prices; our large sales justify a very small profit. Our WATCH REPAIRING is warranted good for 12 months, and universally acknowledged to be A1. Order by mail, or let your friend buy for you. PRINCE & GOLDSMITH, At J. E. SEARS' Drug Store, Public Square, Waco.

HAVE YOU SEEN IT! FREE TO ALL—COME AND SEE! The new addition to the store of LYONS, LINDENTHALL & CO. Makes it the Largest and Most Extensive Dry Goods House in Waco.

Strangers and citizens will find this house always busy selling goods, as our motto is, QUICK SALES AND SMALL PROFITS.

LARGE AND COMPLETE STOCK, A VERY EXTENSIVE STOCK OF WHITE GOODS, MILLINERY AND FANCY GOODS, BOOTS AND SHOES. CLOTHING, HATS AND FURNISHING GOODS. COUNTRY MERCHANTS

LYONS, LINDENTHALL & CO. Waco, Texas, April 28, 1873.

JONES' HACK LINE. WILEY JONES.

S. W. MABRY, Saddle and Harness Maker. Public Square, Waco, Texas.

WM. SIMPSON, WACO, TEXAS. MARBLE YARD.

EAST WACO. KELLUM, ROTAN & CO., WHOLESALE & RETAIL DRY GOODS DEALERS, WACO, TEXAS.

BONNER, CORNISH & CO., Wholesale and Retail Dealers in DRUGS, GROCERIES, Agricultural Implements AND WAGONS, (Near R. R. Depot, East Side River,) BRIDGE AND ELM STREETS, WACO, TEXAS.

WACO. MANUFACTURER Wholesale and Retail Dealer. YOU CAN ALWAYS BUY CHARTER OAK STOVES. FRED. QUARLES, Waco, Texas.

PRINCE & GOLDSMITH, Wholesale and Retail Dealers in Fine Gold and Silver Watches. DIAMONDS, Solid Silver and Plated Ware, Emblem Pins, CLOCKS, Spectacles, Pocket Cutlery, &c. At Sears' Drug Store, Waco.

PROPERTY FOR SALE. SPEIGHT & ELGIN.

WACO. WINN, WALLACE & CO., Auctioneers And General Commission, Receiving & Forwarding Merchants, WACO, TEXAS.

DOWNS, PIERCE & CO., Auctioneers, Gen'l Commission Merchants and Land Agents, Waco, Texas. Cash Advances. Prompt Remittances.

C. N. ALEXANDER & CO., WACO, TEXAS, Cotton Factors.

P. J. PETERS, Manufacturer of Saddlery, Harness, Collars and BUFFALO-SHOES.

A GOOD CHANCE TO BUY Valuable City Property!

A. FURRER, Austin Avenue, Waco, Texas. Dealer in Paints, Oils, Glass, Wall Paper, Window Shades, &c. HOUSE AND SIGN PAINTING!

BATTLE, FICKLEN & CO., Wholesale and Retail Dealers in HARDWARE, GROCERIES, WINES AND LIQUORS. Bridge Street, Waco, Texas.

Waco Daily Advance for May 29, 1873, one of the oldest extant newspapers in Waco. *The Texas Collection, via the Baylor University Libraries Digital Collections.*

This cannot have been what a rowdy Waco crowd wanted to hear, but as Herring points out, it was only a foretaste of the bitter pill that post-Appomattox Wacoans would have to swallow. In the immediate aftermath of the Civil War, Herring notes that "wild anarchy prevailed. The law was impotent." He cites the presence of "sleek-looking, well-clad" Union soldiers in the city and documents a case where a train of oxen and cotton-laden wagons belonging to citizens of the Texas cities of Jefferson and Bonham was "forcibly taken and appropriated. Resistance was vain; and there was no legal address."

Fortunately for Waco—and its many returning Confederate veterans—the situation improved, as "the mechanic, the artisan and the manufacturer were in demand; and soon the merchant had a brisk and profitable trade," Herring notes. But as the economy slowly came back to life thanks to the ranching and cotton industries, there remained distrust and outright apathy on the part of the only partially reformed former Confederates living in Waco during Reconstruction. Herring adds that it took "urgent entreaties and persistent efforts" on the part of Richard Coke's friends and colleagues to convince him to accept a commission as a judge; Coke would go on to serve as governor of Texas from 1874 to 1876.

Herring's write-up contains firsthand information about the events surrounding the building of the Waco Suspension Bridge, one of the most recognizable symbols of the city and a key to its post–Civil War economic recovery. The Waco Bridge Company was chartered in 1866 and began construction of the bridge in October 1868. Herring describes the difficult birth of the bridge in these terms:

> *The material had to be hauled from the then-terminus of the Central Railroad. With all the obstacles that had to be surmounted, without machine shops or foundries, with unskilled labor, relying upon subscriptions of stock that were not promptly paid; and by the bank of Flint & Chamberlin, at one time carrying for the Bridge Company as much as $47,000, President Flint, by his indomitable energy, finesse and perseverance, had our wire Suspension Bridge, with a span cross the Brazos River of 24x495 feet, opened for travel on the 6th day of January, 1870, and fully completed in June following…The first person who crossed over it after completion was Miss Kate Ross, daughter of the old pioneer, Captain S.P. Ross. She was selected for this honor because she was the first white child born in McLennan County.*

Herring goes on to detail the creation of a Waco Tap Railroad, which eventually became part of the Houston and Texas Central Railway Company; the coming of the telegraph; the growth of commercial banks; and the growth of the local newspaper industry. ("At the close of the war there was no newspaper in Waco. Now we have two dailies, three weeklies and two monthlies.")

Herring had high praise for a prominent Wacoan whose name now graces a major city street: Joseph Warren Speight. Herring singled him out for his "more than ordinary executive talent and administrative ability…positive character and unflagging energy," whose service in the educational life of Waco included terms as president of the Waco Female Seminary (later renamed Waco Female College) and Waco University (which would merge with Baylor University in 1885). He was also described as a "bright light in Masonry, [who] has done more than any other person to build up that ancient and honorable fraternity in Waco."

As to the social aspects of life in 1876 Waco, Herring notes:

> *Waco has a Hebrew Association proverbial for the devotion of its members and its charity dispensed. She also has two Masonic Lodges with large and honorable memberships; a Royal Arch Chapter and a Commandery of Knights Templar; an Odd Fellows Lodge of about one hundred and sixty-five members and three Past Grand Masters, and two members who are Representatives from the Grand Lodge of this State to the Grand Lodge of the United States…besides a lodge of Knights of Pythias, Young Men's Christian Association, and several other orders.*

The write-up ends on a hopeful note, with Herring detailing the improvements in housing visible all over the city and touting the fact that "Waco has steadily pursued the 'even tenor of her way,' in substantial and material improvement." He mentions that there are no hard feelings on the part of former Confederates toward their newly arrived Union fellow citizens: "All, ALL our citizens, without reference to their nationality or place of birth, are esteemed and patronized in their business according to their personal merit and moral worth."

Herring's final words could be the rallying cry for all who have sought to document some portion of Waco's history since 1849 and seem a fitting way to end this first chapter of part I:

> *With such a community; with such a beautiful and healthy locality; with such a history; with such a large extent of fertile country tributary to Waco, if her citizens are true to themselves, judging the future by the past, who can foretell the brilliant future that awaits her, or even what may be accomplished in the next decade?*

Herring's words were delivered to a huge crowd of celebrants at Waco's American Centennial celebration on July 4, 1876, and reprinted in the *Waco Register* on July 8. An editorial that ran in the same issue took the opportunity to point out that Herring and others who spoke on the occasion were associated with the Democratic Party, and therefore their views could be seen as being divergent from those held by pro-Union, Republican or non-Confederate sources. However, the author of the *Register* editorial believed that "the intentions of the gentlemen was evidently to make their productions strictly non-political, and they so well succeeded that we feel little disposition to criticize." In fact, Herring's speech was singled out for keeping "on high grounds, and is commendable in tone and spirit." This is high praise for a speech delivered a mere decade after the end of the Civil War to a crowd that included Confederate veterans and reformed secessionists, especially when it was delivered on America's one-hundredth birthday celebration.

2

Waco Celebrates the American Centennial

The occasion that impelled M.D. Herring to put pen to paper in 1876 was the celebration of the American centennial, a nationwide opportunity to cast the recently reunited country's attention back to its glorious roots in the American Revolution and to reignite a common sense of purpose and identity following the devastation of the Civil War. In a city located in the reconstructing South, it would have been understandable for Waco's citizenry to pay little heed to what could easily be cast as a Federal holiday or to harbor resentment for the significant number of people there who were new arrivals from Northern cities. But by all accounts, Waco's celebration of the centennial was a jubilant, appropriate and—if press accounts are to be believed—lengthy affair that demonstrated how much progress had been made in healing the wounds of the Civil War.

An advertisement for the celebratory parade ran for several days in the *Waco Daily Examiner* under a headline featuring a single year: 1876! The ad spelled out the "programme" for the day, as well as the official participants in the parade and the members of the various committees that planned the day's events. According to the ad, the program's agenda was:

> *1. 13 Guns by Artillery corps*
> *2. Music at Rostrum*
> *3. Introductory remarks by the President* [Dr. Thomas Moore]
> *4. Prayer by the Chaplain, R.C. Burleson, D.D.*
> *5. Music by the Choir*

6. Reading of the Declaration of Independence, by W.L. Prather
7. Salute by Waco Grays
8. Music by Stoddard's Cornet Band
9. Oration by Col. G.B. Gerald
10. Refreshments
11. After refreshment 13 regular toasts to be announced by the President; thereafter volunteer toasts promiscuously
12. Music by the Choir at rostrum
13. Historical essays
14. Music by the choir

The day began with a scene of orderly chaos, as thousands of revelers showed up at the public square hoping to take part in the opening procession. According to the write-up in the July 8, 1876 issue of the *Waco Register*, the crowd was so large that "the procession was so much longer than the distance to be marched to—the Fair Grounds—a mile and a half." Through the process of organizing the throngs into a semblance of order, the paper reported, "So great was the multitude and so much time did it take to arrange even the bulk of it into order, that the head of the procession did not find itself at the gates of the grounds till after 12 o'clock, while the rear was still being organized in Waco."

Ad for Waco's centennial of American independence in the *Waco Daily Examiner*, July 2, 1876. *The Texas Collection, via the Baylor University Libraries Digital Collections.*

The procession included a who's who of local dignitaries, including the leadership of the various planning committees; the mayor of Waco, the city council and various officials; the Waco Fire Department; floats representing "industries on wheels" and "the Press"; "38 young ladies on horseback, representing the 38 States of the Union"; and "citizens in vehicles, on horseback and on foot."

According to the *Register* article documenting the festivities, there were a number of floats representing various local industries, the "largest and most conspicuous" being that of the Star Iron Works. The *Examiner* described it this way:

> *An engine with smoke stack and all, and a large cotton gin and other machinery were mounted on a huge wagon with the engine fired up and the machinists all at work—the frame work of the wagon being beautifully ornamented with flags.*

So great was the spirit of bonhomie on that day that the *Register* even had nice words to say about one of its rival newspapers, the *Waco Daily Examiner*. The *Register* reporter noted,

> *Our city contemporary, the "Examiner," also under a beautifully formed canopy of red, white and blue, moved out with press all in working order, and printers, and throwing off as they passed along a very interesting Centennial issue of the "Examiner," the sheets of which were eagerly seized by the crowd as they were thrown off. We had the pleasure of standing up and singing the "Star Spangled Banner" out of this edition of the "Examiner."*

Once the procession reached the fairgrounds, a slew of addresses, prayers and other public oratory took place in the broiling July heat. A "grand barbecue entertainment" lunch was held, but the amount available was insufficient to feed the massive crowds, so people who lived closer to town went home for lunch and "surrendered the pleasure of partaking" to those who came "from the country farther away." After lunch came the toasts—and there were many in which to participate, judging by the list printed in the *Register*:

> 1. *The day we celebrate* [July 4th]
> 2. *The immortal memory of him who was first in war, first in peace, and first in the hearts of his countrymen* [George Washington]
> 3. *The Constitution of the United States, the source of our national greatness, the palladium of our liberties*
> 4. *Our patriot sires of '76: all honor to their memories*
> 5. *Thomas Jefferson, the Apostle of American Liberty*
> 6. *Andrew Jackson, the hero of Chalmette, and the second Washington*
> 7. *The freedom of the press, may it never be abridged*
> 8. *Habeas Corpus, the great writ of right, may it ever be held sacred*
> 9. *The hero of San Jacinto, the Father of Texas* [Sam Houston]
> 10. *Our own loved Lone Star State, as she is in territory so may she be in numbers, wealth and intelligence the Empire State of the Union*

11. The American Union, may it ever be perpetuated in the spirit of its founders
12. Woman—Heaven's last best gift to man—may she ever be cherished and protected by the gallant sons of noble sires
13. Our country, our whole country, the land of the free and the home of the brave

Thirteen toasts for thirteen original colonies, and no word of discord or division to be found, though the *Register* points out the "toasts were read beneath a scorching sun, and the responses were brief." The event was capped off by fireworks and more music from local bands, and a ball was held at the McClelland House.

A curious note regarding the local bands is related in the *Register* article. Despite the huge numbers of Wacoans and McLennan County residents taking place in the procession—including two local bands, Stoddard's and Hathaway's—the article points out, "The colored band, in splendid uniform, were out, [but] by some mistake did not get a place in the procession. This is to be regretted." The article continues, "As the band plays well and is finely uniformed and could have contributed music somewhere in the line of march. We do not think the omission was intentional." Given the documented violence and intimidation aimed at African Americans across Texas and the South following the Civil War, the "accidental" omission of a black marching band from the day's festivities is another example of the uneasy—and unequal—truce being navigated by those who lived in the Reconstruction South.

Overall, the documentation on the American centennial in Waco points to a unified, exuberant and suitably patriotic affair punctuated by a rather ominous display of what looks to be casual racism toward an African American band. It is, therefore, a fitting metaphor for the overall arc of history in this period, when the white majority sought to find meaning and healing in the wake of a devastating conflict, but the people at the center of that conflict—the newly freed former slaves—saw their freedom coming with a heavy burden yet to bear in the form of everyday discrimination, both overt and undercover. That oppression would only grow more egregious, as we will see with several stories documented in part III.

3
"Geyser City"
Artesian Wells and the Water Cure

Ask anyone who's ever tried to coax a living from the land, and they'll tell you the one nonnegotiable element to a successful harvest is water. The same is true for anyone looking to develop a thriving community, and if you want to establish a nineteenth-century health equivalent to the gold rush, it helps to have access to vast quantities of fresh, easily accessible "liquid gold." Fortunately for early Wacoans, the presence of large stores of water just underneath their feet—to say nothing of the Brazos River, which forms the city's northern/western boundaries—meant not only the opportunity to create an ever-growing population base but made the perfect setting for Waco to become part of the water cure craze of the late nineteenth century as well.

Waco came of age at the precise time of the rise in popularity of the "water cure" (or hydropathy or, in today's terms, hydrotherapy) in the United States. Though its roots extend back to ancient times, the concept of "taking the waters" found new heights of popularity in Europe in the 1840s and came to America shortly thereafter. At the height of the cure's popularity, hydropathy adherents claimed relief from a wide range of maladies from the common (Backaches! The grippe! Upset stomach!) to the wildly improbable (cancer, paralysis and mental illness, to name a few). Towns like Mineral Wells near Fort Worth, Texas, or Hot Springs, Arkansas, became hot spots for people seeking relief from their ailments or simply an opportunity to lounge in heated mineral water in an early version of a hot tub or Jacuzzi.

The basic belief of the pro-hydropathy camp came down to the understanding that waters trapped below the earth's surface were infused with minerals that had seeped into them during their journey through the upper layers of the soil and down into the reservoirs, where they collected in vast pools. The waters were subjected to subterranean heat, which amplified the healing properties of the minerals until the waters were released back up to the surface either by means of an underground stimulus or when tapped into by a well drilled from the surface. Taking those waters and heating them in tubs, inhaling their vapors or simply drinking them was believed to provide medicinal benefits for all but the most infirm.

Waco's discovery of its artesian wealth dates back to March 10, 1889, when Captain J.D. Bell struck an underground reservoir after drilling 1,830 feet down, in an area now known appropriately as Bell's Hill. According to an article in the March 18, 1892 *Waco Morning News*, it was his "unusual display of perseverance and commendable zeal" that led to the discovery of a hot reservoir of "crystal fluid." By 1892, there would be sixteen "developed" wells across Waco, some drilled within feet of one another and others spread apart at distances of up to four miles.

Photo of derrick and associated buildings at the site of the first artesian well drilled on Bell's Hill in 1889. *Lee Lockwood Library and Museum.*

THE DAY: WACO, TEXAS. SATURDAY, AUGUST 23. 5

SYRUP of FIGS

Local Time Card.

AN ADDRESS

Waco.

THE GEYSER CITY

WACO, TEX.

The Capital City of Central Texas and the Fertile Brazos Valley Region, Which Furnishes One-Fifth of the World's Cotton Supply.

WACO CITY.

Population	25,000
Taxable Values	$10,000,000
Manufacturing Investments	$800,000

M'LENNAN COUNTY.

Population	50,000
Taxable Values	$17,000,000
Miles of Railway in County	160
Value Agricultural Products last year	$3,000,000

The Waco Artesian Wells are not equalled in the world for volume, power and value of the water.

CITY AND COUNTY PRESENT Most Favorable Opportunities for Investment of Capital and Especially in Manufacturing and for Business Enterprise and Industry.

THE DAY WILL CHEERFULLY answer all inquiries about Waco or McLennan County and furnish practical and reliable information free of cost. Address,

THE DAY, WACO, TEXAS.

SCHENCK'S MANDRAKE PILLS

ERRORS OF YOUTH.

HEALTH IS WEALTH

MALYDOR

ABBOTT'S EAST INDIAN CORN PAINT

Ad for promoting Waco as the "Geyser City," from the *Day* newspaper, August 23, 1890. *The Texas Collection, via the Baylor University Libraries Digital Collections.*

The article goes on to excerpt information from a report by Colonel S.H. Pope, secretary of the Waco Board of Trade:

> *Why is Waco called the Geyser City of Texas? Because of its artesian wells and phenomenal heat of their waters. Why is Waco the Geyser city of America? It has the greatest number of overflowing wells of any city on this continent, and can show a well, whose daily output, initial pressure and heat exceed that of any in America or Europe.... Probably no event of such far reaching effect has occurred in the history of Waco, as the discovery of hot water and the development of a number of artesian wells, phenomenal in heat, output and initial pressure.... The water is soft and almost chemically pure, the minerals held in suspension are imponderable and without taste. It is used for mechanical and domestic purposes. It possesses remedial properties equal to any of the thermal springs of America.**

Not everyone was ready to buy into Waco's baptism-by-artesian-waters approach to statewide prominence, however. A former Wacoan named Bartow, who had once written for the *Waco Examiner* before heading to Victoria to edit a paper there, was reported in the April 9, 1889 edition of the *Waco Morning News* as saying, "Waco cackles over the artesian wells much as a young hen does her first and only egg. It is very touching, and also a great pity she has not something of more importance to boom on."

According to a report in the March 23, 1915 *Waco Morning News*, by that point in the city's history, more than half of the water being used in Waco came from artesian wells. The article notes, "All of the territory south of Webster street is supplied entirely from artesian wells and half of the water used north of Webster is from the same source." The increased demands for artesian water spurred from regular consumption and new water-related businesses alike. Ads for "electrified artesian water" were being hocked in local newspapers well into the late 1920s, and an 1894 *Culler's Guide to the City of Waco* predicted, "The day is not far distant when the annual financial benefits to the city and its citizens—derived from invalid visitors seeking

* In a charming example of how randomly assembled nineteenth-century newspapers often prove to be, the next article below Pope's "Geyser City" report states, "Deputy Constable Harry Crowder had the misfortune yesterday of being kicked on the hand by his horse. No bones were broken, the back of the hand is badly bruised and lacerated from which today he is suffering much pain." One wonders what Deputy Crowder thought of having his injuries reported into the public record in this manner.

health and a more congenial climate—will equal or exceed the value of the largest cotton crop ever raised in McLennan County."

One of the most important and architecturally interesting examples of Waco's artesian water–based economy was the Waco Natatorium (or the Natatorio-Sanitorium, or Natatorium Hotel, depending on the time you asked someone its name), opened in 1892 by a Confederate army veteran named Robert Parrott. According to the Natatorium's write-up on the Waco History website, the site for the building at Fourth and Mary was chosen due to its proximity to the center of town and, importantly, the Cotton Belt depot, which would allow travelers through town a chance to use its services during a layover.

The Natatorium's original building lasted only a little over a year before burning in 1894. The successor building was envisioned as something much grander at four stories tall with a rooftop garden and a unique Spanish-influenced architecture that set it apart from other buildings constructed in this era. According to Miller's article,

> *The Natatorium was equipped with departments for both ladies and gentlemen to have Turkish and Russian baths, individual baths, tubs, vapor rooms, sweat and resting rooms, furnished rooms, a cafe, offices, and parlors. The Natatorium also had one of the largest indoor swimming pools in the South....One room of the building was known to have dozens of pairs of crutches left behind by people who came to the Natatorium needing the walking aids when they came in, but no longer needing them after soaking in the baths.*

By the mid-1920s, Waco's artesian wells were in a rapidly diminishing state. The area was in the midst of a devastating drought by 1925, and the city debated how to solve the problem—a contentious issue that involved an option to dam the Bosque River to create a reserve of storm waters to use during dry periods. By 1926, "the city's artesian wells were being blown with compressed air to make them produce more water," according to an October 26, 1975 article in the *Waco Tribune-Herald*: "The water commission was concerned that Waco's underground supply of water, once considered to be limitless, was disappearing."

An article in the *Waco News-Tribune* of August 25, 1926, paints a bleak picture for the future of the artesian wells:

> *Gradual failure of the artesian water supply of Waco was discussed in a statement given out yesterday from Bosque Lake Information headquarters,*

> *in the Raleigh Hotel. The statement called attention to the fact that artesian wells, when first brought in here 37 years ago, had sufficient force to gust 200 feet into the air. The engineers' report to the water board was quoted, in which a chart shows the output of the First Street Artesian wells decreasing from 2,000,000 gallons a day in 1918 to three-quarters of a million gallons a day in 1925. The Vermont Street wells were shown to have fallen off from 1,000,000 gallons a day in 1916 to 500,000 gallons per day last year.*

The report is further quoted as follows:

> *All efforts to bring back this falling supply by cleaning and shooting these wells have resulted in failure. The data indicates that these wells are drawing from an underground reservoir and that it is being gradually emptied. Though there may be an inflow to this reservoir, the data indicates that the rate of inflow at the present time is far less than the amount of water being taken out.... The records indicate that additional wells would increase the supply for only a short period of time until the immediate vicinity is drained.*

The article ends on an ominous note: "The experience of Waco with artesian wells has been similar to that of other cities using artesian water. As the city grew and the demand increased, the supply from wells has almost always dropped down until some other source of supply was necessary."

By 1926, the depleted state of the artesian wells led to the closure of the Waco Natatorium, a fixture on the local hydro scene since its original structure opened in 1892. Despite wells drilled to an initial depth of 1,850 feet, the flow of artesian water dried up, and the Natatorium closed in December 1926, according to the write-up on the Waco History website. The building burned on January 1, 1927, and was never rebuilt.

Attempts in 1927 to pump air into as many as eight wells in the hope of increasing production were only partially successful, but advertisements in Waco newspapers continued to tout access to artesian water as a selling point, such as this ad from the October 6, 1928 *Waco News-Tribune*: "FOR RENT—Three unfurnished rooms, private home, lights, water, gas, artesian water, $10 per month. 3500 Ethel."

The artesian wells experienced a brief return to importance in the early 1950s when Waco experienced another of its periodic episodes of drought. This time, according to an April 4, 1952 article in the *Waco News-Tribune*, city officials were exploring bringing the wells back into production to "help meet an anticipated shortage. The water board recently authorized [Water Superintendent Hubert] Davis to make tests and connect the artesian wells to the city system to meet demands expected to increase soon."

Over time, commercial water supplies from sources like the Brazos River and, later, Lake Waco came to supplant the importance of Waco's artesian wells. Almost all were capped off and forgotten in the mid-twentieth century, but a few persisted for a few years more. One notable example likely fed a fountain located at the corner of Jefferson Avenue and University Parks Drive, known locally as La Pila ("the basin"). In 2017, archaeologists and volunteers began excavations at La Pila, which was important to the Calle Dos ("Second Street" or "Two Street") neighborhood until it was capped in 1950 and buried under fill dirt during urban renewal, according to an article by J.B. Smith in the *Waco Tribune-Herald*. Evidence from a 1933 *Tribune-Herald* story indicates the fountain was fed by an artesian well sunk nearby. As of this writing, local Hispanic museum leaders and archaeologists are hoping to restore La Pila as part of an ongoing effort to showcase Hispanic history and culture in Waco.

The former La Pila fountain site in the early stages of archaeological discovery operations. *Author's collection.*

A fine example of a preserved artesian well can still be seen if one visits the Dr Pepper Museum and Free Enterprise Institute, housed in the former Artesian Bottling & Manufacturing building, the first commercial bottling plant for Dr Pepper in Waco. One of the local wells was used in the production of Dr Pepper, and until it was ordered capped in 1928, it remained an integral part of the process. Today, the well is covered with a thick glass cover that allows visitors to see down more than twenty-five feet into the Waco soil.

Waco's time in the artesian well health and wellness community lasted less than thirty years, and unlike Mineral Wells, which has experienced a renaissance of sorts around the bottling of its locally produced "Crazy Water," Waco has made no concerted efforts to revisit its hydropathy heritage. Perhaps, given the local interest in downtown revitalization in recent years, someone with a bent for entrepreneurism could reestablish a Natatorium Hotel and offer "the baths" in Waco again for the first time in a century. Surely plenty of nostalgic Wacoans would be willing to (pardon the expression) jump right in.

4

The Tantalizing (and Disastrous) Dream of Steamboats on the Brazos

With Waco's growing importance as a commercial and business hub in the late nineteenth century, various entrepreneurs and entities harbored a secret dream: to see regular steamboat traffic powering up and down the Brazos River from Waco to the Gulf of Mexico, a virtual pipeline of raw material exports and finished goods imports that could be plied by anyone with a suitable craft and the will to succeed. There was only one problem with this vision of a water-based economy: the river itself. Due to the nature of the Brazos's course between Waco and the Gulf, there existed a series of low points, rocky shoals and waterfalls between Waco and a spot in Milam County (referred to as "Old Fort Sullivan" in a 1905 *Waco Weekly Tribune* article) that made the first seventy-five miles of such a journey downstream extremely difficult in the best conditions and impossible for most of the year.

But that doesn't mean people weren't willing to try, as the *Weekly Tribune* article points out with two specific examples: the *Kate Ross* and the *Lizzie Fisher*. The article, reproduced in the Summer 1971 issue of *Waco Heritage & History*, points out the efforts undertaken by the two boats' creators to strike it rich with a Brazos-friendly transportation system that could take Waco's bountiful output to the world via the port at Galveston, while bringing in the finest things produced by countries the world over.

The earliest example of a proper Waco steamboat was the vessel that came to be known under the name *Kate Ross*. The *Tribune* article writer points out that the concept for the *Kate Ross* sprang from the mind of a man named Gibson (first name not recorded), who had "steamboated on the lower Brazos, [and] was residing temporarily" in Waco. He convinced a number of Wacoans to partner with him, including brothers Norman and Harvey Conger, whose jointly owned machine shop provided the engines, while two other brothers, Tom and William Leonard, served as contractors and shipbuilders. Gibson provided half the money and commenced building the ship in the early autumn of 1874.

The *Tribune* article described its construction and design thusly:

> *His* [Gibson's] *"ship yard" for building was on the east bank of the river, at a point on the hill but near the stream. By the end of 1874, he launched the hull and then proceeded to put on the lower deck and what he called a "hurricane deck," but it was a flat roof and could be used on occasion for dancing. The boat was about one hundred feet long and twenty-five feet beam, with a hull six feet deep, drawing not over sixteen inches of water light. The boat was of the stern wheel order, and a well-built, staunch craft, was painted white and as it sat at the foot of Washington Street presented a neat appearance.*

When it came time to christen the boat, Gibson chose a name that was certain to bring approval from the Waco citizenry. Kate Ross was the first white child born in what became McLennan County, and she was married to Tom Padgitt—a well-known and prosperous local merchant—and her father was Shapely P. Ross, a local legend, pioneer and soldier. Under this auspicious name, the *Kate Ross* made its maiden voyage in February 1875 roughly seven miles upriver, carrying a "numerous and merry party of Wacoites," including Governor Richard Coke (a Wacoan), who "came here from Austin for the event and on the trip at the river made a glowing speech." Music, dancing and positive press coverage surrounded the *Kate Ross*'s initial foray, which was deemed a success.

Still, pleasure cruises wouldn't pay the bills for Captain Gibson, so he began making a series of runs to a small town roughly thirty miles upriver called Towash. Situated near present-day Lake Whitney, Towash was home to a "splendid flouring mill and several stores," as well as a post office, and it served as the "center of a prosperous agricultural community." Gibson saw a business opportunity in making runs to Towash to bring back goods to Waco, namely, "cotton, flour, hides and cedar charcoal," which the *Tribune* article points out was "fairly profitable" work.

Gibson had never planned to make short runs out of Waco as his final business opportunity, as he hoped to make a living plying trade on the lower Brazos between Brazoria and Columbia. The *Tribune* article notes that his plan was to outfit the boat with a cabin for passengers and other upgrades suitable for river commerce at Galveston, then put back into the Brazos at Indianola and begin making commercial runs. There was only one thing standing in the way of Gibson's best-laid plans, an impediment that exists to this very day: the "falls" in the river, located in the appropriately named Falls County. In the 1870s, the only way for a boat to make it through the falls and to the lower Brazos was during a stage of high flood, and even then, the situation was tricky for the most experienced pilots.

Knowing this, Gibson hired a pilot named Tom Jennings to help make the push over the falls. All he needed was a suitable flood, which arrived in June 1875, in an event the locals called a "red rise" for the color the river took on as its volume swelled and red dirt from upstream influenced its color. Gibson said goodbye to Waco and set out for Falls County, and as the *Tribune* writer points out, "The 'Kate Ross' was never seen here again." For a description of the remainder of the *Kate Ross*'s final days, it is worth extensively quoting a passage that Captain Jennings related to the *Tribune*:

> *"We got away from Waco," said Captain Jennings, "all right and as we thought there was ample water for the undertaking we were enthusiastic. Gibson told me all his plans about getting the boat ready for the fall trade in the lower Brazos and I was to be his pilot, at a good salary. We got as far as the falls of the Brazos and then found the river was falling more rapidly than we had calculated, but we got over and went on to the next falls, opposite Calvert* [in] *Robertson County. There our boat met disaster, for she stuck, right on the falls. About a third of the craft was over the falls, but as the engines, the weighty part, was a little further back, there was no danger of going over. We stuck there ten days and one day the river rose a foot or so and we passed over safely.*
>
> *We pursued our way down the river to what was then known as Smiley's Ferry, opposite or near the town of Calvert. The river was falling again and we lodged on a shoal. The boat never got off that shoal. Weeks and weeks she lay there. Had we had even one more foot of water we would have got over safely enough. We grew discouraged. I needed to work and could not wait any longer, so I bade Capt. Gibson goodbye and went on to Galveston. He remained with his boat a couple of weeks and then he, too—so I heard*

> *afterward—gave up the fight and left her. What disposition was made of the boat I never knew, except that she was broken up and the timbers and lumber sold. The Conger brothers came down there to look after their interest in the machinery.*

Captain Jennings cited the lack of an additional foot or so of water as the seemingly minor need that kept the *Kate Ross* from living a viable life as a trading ship on the lower Brazos. He notes that the lack of a railroad between Galveston and Central Texas meant a profit could be made moving goods up and down the river, and that "there was plenty of freight for several boats on the lower river, and let me tell you the Brazos from Old Washington to the gulf is a fine boating stream." Sadly for Captain Gibson, his dreams died in Robertson County, dashed on the shoals of wasted opportunity.

The story of the *Lizzie Fisher*, the only other steamboat worthy of the name to originate in Waco, is perhaps the more fascinating of the two, due mostly to its mysterious denouement. The facts as laid out in the *Tribune* article are that the boat was smaller than the *Kate Ross* by a goodly margin and was built near the suspension bridge in 1875 by a man named Woodruff, who locals might have remembered as "a small, slim, sallow complected [*sic*] man, who bragged a great deal of his little river boat and how she could 'cut the water.'" Woodruff announced that he planned to make runs to Towash similar to the early excursions of the *Kate Ross*, but low water levels prevented him from doing so, to the point that it was alleged his creditors were getting antsy and that Woodruff was "pretty deep in debt." The situation was tense, as Woodruff and his wife and two children lived aboard the *Lizzie Fisher*, crammed into its tiny cabin, awaiting a chance to depart Waco for more profitable stretches of the river.

A sudden red rise hit the Waco area without warning in July 1875—just a month after the one that had given the *Kate Ross* its chance to escape—and a "booming" Brazos River swept through town. The next morning, the *Lizzie Fisher* was gone. Stories began to swirl that the ship and all aboard had been swept away in the flood and its wreckage had been found downstream along with several bodies claimed to be those of Captain Woodruff and his family. These stories were never substantiated, however, and before long a new set of stories began to circulate based on reports from "Waco people" who had been in New Orleans a few months after the red rise of July 1875. These unnamed Wacoans claimed they had seen the *Lizzie Fisher* in the Crescent City and that the boat had arrived there by means of navigating the swollen Brazos to the Gulf of Mexico before braving the passage to New Orleans.

Corroborating this story was a lawyer's reporting to the *Tribune* that shortly after the *Lizzie Fisher* disappeared from Waco, money began to arrive to pay off its creditors—"it was $200 or $300"—adding credence to the fact that while the *Lizzie Fisher* may not have made it to New Orleans, it at least made it to profitability somewhere.

The *Tribune* article on the *Lizzie Fisher* and the *Kate Ross* ends with a prediction that would not come to pass despite on-again, off-again efforts to make it so. The writer ends his story with a paragraph full of high hopes:

> *For it is likely to come to pass that the Brazos—which the people of the town were wont to regard as a nuisance rather than otherwise, since it was not navigable and needed the expense of ferries first and later, bridges; with its damaging and worrying inundations, that at times have driven people from their homes and destroyed valuable crops—it may be the compensation of the future that this stream so long useless save as a fertilizing agent as the Nile is for the farm lands along its banks, will be the prime factor in creating a city that will be the peer in all respects of any in the state.*

The writer's prophecy is only half-wrong, however, in that it misidentifies the source of the boom in Waco's transportation-based prosperity as river-bound, rather than steam-driven on rails of steel. For the coming of the railroad would indeed open the city to markets far beyond its Central Texas location, and a rise in the quality of life would accompany the iron horses that began to roll into Waco as the nineteenth century bled into the twentieth just a few short years after the untimely ends of the *Kate Ross* and the *Lizzie Fisher*, the only homemade steamboats ever fated to grace the Brazos.

5

William Cowper Brann

Sinner's Saint, False Prophet or Journalistic Crusader?

In many ways, the late nineteenth century media landscape bears some striking similarities to today. Where today's news can be delivered from a major media conglomerate or a "citizen journalist" pumping out articles on a local blog, news in late 1800s Waco could come from a number of daily, weekly or monthly newspapers, each with its own slant on the news and a dedicated reader base eager to hear not only the goings-on around town but also the opinions of the editor behind each edition. And much like today, where the loudest voices often gather the highest ratings—and, therefore, the lion's share of the advertising profits—the news business in 1890s Waco would come to be dominated by one voice that rose loudest of all: that of William Cowper Brann, the publisher of the *Iconoclast*.

The details of William Cowper Brann's life are well documented in a variety of places, so we will not spend much time retreading well-trod ground here. A quick sketch of his life would include his birth in 1855 to a Presbyterian minister father; a transient early life spent in numerous cities, including St. Louis, Galveston, Houston and San Antonio; his discovery that he enjoyed writing and had a gift for prose (though it was often quite sharp and purple); a marriage that produced three children; and the establishment of his "journal of personal protest," which he named the *Iconoclast*, first circulated in 1891 in Austin (where it flopped) and again in 1894 in Waco (where it reached a peak circulation of some 100,000 people). It was this last achievement that gave Brann his notoriety and led to a series of violent events in Waco that ultimately spelled his doom courtesy of an enraged Baylor supporter and a Colt single-action army revolver.

But before we get to his death by assassination in broad daylight, it is important to paint a picture of the man Brann was and the worldview he presented in the pages of his inflammatory publication. According to Dayton Kelley's entry on Brann in *The Handbook of Waco and McLennan County, Texas*:

> *Brann's writing style was unique: an imaginative blending of the beautiful with the banal and barbaric, poetic tenderness with cow-lot crudity, supported throughout by lightning flashes of original thought, philosophy, and wit. But as the title implied, Brann took obvious pleasure in directing stinting attacks upon institutions and persons he considered to be hypocritical or overly sanctimonious. Among such was Waco's renowned Baylor University, which he scourged as "a great storm center of misinformation." He by no means confined his distaste to Baptists and was especially keen to express his dislike of Episcopalians, anything British, and perhaps his greatest vitriol was reserved for African Americans.*

An equal-opportunity attacker with a broad range of targets paints a picture of a man with a whole shed full of axes to grind, but reading Brann's words with a critical eye reveals the winking smile behind many of the pointed barbs, and it can often seem that his cruelest jabs are made in an exaggerated manner so as to make difficult points go down easier. A reader's indignance over a crass turn of phrase could cause that same reader to spend more time contemplating the deeper meaning of Brann's words and, if Brann were lucky, lead that reader to embrace his larger point. (Or so the theory goes, at least. For there were plenty of passages where Brann seems to be writing cruelly for the simple pleasure of being cruel, and it can often be difficult to suss out the difference.)

Before he settled down in Waco in 1894, Brann made several appearances as a guest lecturer, expounding on various topics of interest to Gilded Age tastes. An article in the February 23, 1892 *Waco Morning News* sheds some light on his orations:

> *An Intellectual Treat: Mr. W.C. Brann, editor of the "Iconoclast," lectured last night, according to previous announcement, at the city hall to a large and appreciative audience upon the subject of the Modern Mokanna. The hall was crowded to overflowing and the lecture was one continued strain of*

> *eloquence from the start to the finish, holding his audience spell bound* [sic] *throughout. It is not saying too much to assert that a Waco audience has never before enjoyed such an intellectual treat as that listened to last night and it has ever since been the subject of favorable comment from all who heard it. His subject tonight will be "Humbugs." Admission free.*

Brann's subject that night points to his eclectic tastes and ability to weave together an attention-grabbing narrative on even the most arcane of subjects. The Mokanna was a character from an 1817 Thomas Moore poem, itself based loosely on a self-proclaimed Persian prophet named al-Muqanna or "The Veiled One." Mokanna became a central figure in a Masonic group based out of St. Louis called the Mystic Order of Veiled Prophets of the Enchanted Realm. Brann spent time in St. Louis as a young man, so it is possible he first heard of the Mokanna during his time there. It is likely that the "modern Mokanna" referred to in Brann's speech is Mark Hanna, a political ally of William McKinley whom Brann lambasted in print as the "Vampire of Poverty, the Attilla [*sic*] of Industry, the Avatar of Greed, the Scourge of God." In that article, he refers to Hannah as "a modern Mokanna." Thus, he was able to entertain a Waco crowd by drawing parallels between a Persian prophet, a Masonic secret society and a Republican political kingmaker—all for the reasonable price of people's time and attention.

Brann's magnetism extended beyond his ability to charm a crowd with his words. In a 1954 article recounting the life of Mrs. W.B. Knight—then the oldest member of the Waco Press Club—the subject gives the reporter her impressions of Brann, whom she met when he was editing the *Iconoclast*. "Brann was a 'precious man,' she recalls. He was tall, lean, rather handsome, devoted to his family, and broken hearted that a reprimand he gave a young daughter, customary for fathers in those days, caused her to take her own life." This is a reference to an incident in which a young boy left flowers at the Brann home for Inez, his twelve-year-old daughter. According to Richard Snow, writing in the Summer 1979 issue of *American Heritage* magazine, Brann accused her of "encouraging her admirer, and, when she denied it, of lying. Shortly afterward, her parents found her dead. A note she had left began, 'Dear Momma: Tomorrow this time I will be dead. I took all of that morphine. I don't want to live. I could never be as good as you want me to.'"

Following his daughter's suicide, the topic of "female purity" became a recurring theme in Brann's writings, but it was by no means his only hobby horse. A look at the table of contents for volume 2 of *Brann, the Iconoclast: A*

Collection of the Writings of W.C. Brann, published in 1898 by his widow, reveals a number of favorite topics:

A Message to Mary
Atheism and Orthodoxy
Cyclones and Sanctification
Christian England and India
Christ Comes to Texas
Catholic vs. Protestant "Cranks"
Dutch, Deity and Devil
Dogmatism the Mother of Doubt
Prayers for the Pagan

And so on. Religion—and his belief that many who practice it were humbugs, hypocrites or worse—was a favorite target. Brann even dreamed up a conversation between himself and Jesus Christ, who comes to visit Brann while the editor is "reading a report of the regular meeting of the Dallas Pastors' Association":

> *There came a gentle rap at his door and a strange figure stood before him. It was that of a man of perhaps three-and-thirty years, barefoot, bareheaded and clothed only in a single garment, much worn and sadly soiled.*
>
> *"Peace to this house," he said, in a voice soft and sweet as that of a well-bred woman. "A cup of cold water, I pray you."*
>
> *"Water? Cert*[ainly]*. Steer yourself against the cooler over there. You look above the Weary Willie business. Sit down until I find a jumping-off place in this article on The Monetary Situation, and perhaps I can fish up a stray quarter that's dodged the foreign mission fund."*
>
> *…He took a dry crust from a leathern wallet, and, blessing it, offered a portion to the editor.*
>
> *"Jesus Christ! You don't eat that, do you?"*
>
> *The visitor rose, a startled look on his face. "You know me, then? Yes, it is I—Jesus of Nazareth. I have walked the earth an entire year, clad as I was eighteen centuries ago, living as I did then, mingling with those called by*

> *my name, conversing with those who profess to teach my doctrine, and none knew me. Nay more: They sometimes spurned me from their doors, and even delivered me to the minions of Caesar as a vagabond. You look incredulous. Behold the nail-prints in my hands and feet, the spear wound in my side, the scars made by the crown of thorns upon my brow."*

This passage reveals both Brann's wicked wit—exclaiming a blasphemy that is instead mistaken for an identification—and his use of descriptive text to point out the hypocrisy of self-professed "Christians" whose attitude and actions do not measure up to their religion's namesake. Another of his tactics was to set up a straw man whose bombastic statement would lead to Brann's exploration of a topic of interest, as in the opening paragraph to his piece "Cyclones and Sanctification":

> *The terrible cyclone which recently tore its way through St. Louis prompted a resident of the stricken city to complain to the* Iconoclast, *that a God of infinite justice and mercy would not indiscriminately destroy saint and sinner by flood and fire, and crush nursing babes beneath an avalanche of stone and brick. Like Jonah, he feels that he does well to be angry, for he declares that if the Deity really exists, he is a demon.*

This passage would be provocative enough, but Brann—never one to keep the pot at a simmer—turns up the rhetoric to a full boil with the remaining lines of the paragraph: "and adds that 'the God idea was born in the stupid brain of negroes on the upper Nile, and from thence o'erspread the planet like a foul pestilence.'"

Passages like this make it easy to see why Brann's invective created so much hard feeling around town, especially among the targets of his wrath. Brann's piece goes on to explore the conflict between natural laws, man's laws and God's laws, but it all starts with a racist slander to get the ball rolling. And like many of his passages, there are flashes of philosophical sophistication, as when Brann discusses the way in which God (the Deity) reveals himself to man:

> *The religious idea is often perverted; yet so far back as we can trace the history of the human race, it has constituted the heart of civilization, the efficient cause of the social compact, the dynamo of the world. I do not mean that foolish fanaticism or blood-thirsty bigotry has been a blessing; they bear the same relation to the moral that cyclones and earthquakes do*

> *to the physical world. I allude to that feeling of moral responsibility which marks the first step of a people from subter-savagery, that concept of duty to what we call the Deity, which leads men to erect altars and supplicate the unseen power. This conscience or soul of men precedes civilization, makes progress possible. As it develops the race advances; as it becomes perverted the race returns to barbarism, carrying with it the adscititious* [sic] *curse of bigotry. God has revealed himself to man—not by laws graven on tables of stone, plates of silver or tables of horn; not by feathered but non-oviparous angels seen in trance-vision by sanctified tramps who trotted about the country peddling hair-trigger curses and sacred hoodoos; but in human life itself. "You touch heaven," says Novalis, "when you lay your hand upon a human body." It is a temple in which dwells a portion of that divine intelligence which is God.*

Quite aside from his musings on the eternal, Brann's full-throated attacks on Baylor University earned him both scorn and support among Waco's population. Support came from those who bore some ill-will toward the Baptist institution of higher education founded in 1845 in Independence, Texas, and moved to Waco in 1885; outrage radiated from all who saw its presence in Waco as beyond a net positive but a sign of the city's educational and spiritual leadership in the state of Texas. So it was no surprise when Brann published a series of high-powered attacks on the university in response to what would become known as the Antonia Texeira affair, and even less surprising that his attacks would ultimately cost him his life.

The basic facts of the Texeira affair are that Antonia was brought to Waco from Brazil by a missionary at the age of eleven; he claimed to have rescued her from a life of despair and debauchery in the home of her mother, a courtesan. The girl was employed as domestic help in the house of Rufus C. Burleson, the president of Baylor at the time. The ultimate goal was to make her well versed in Baptist theology and then return her to Brazil to serve as a counter to the overwhelming Catholic majority. When Texeira was thirteen or fourteen (the records are unclear), it was revealed in the *Waco Morning News* on June 15, 1895, that she was pregnant. She claimed she had been "drugged and raped on multiple occasions by H. Steen Morris, brother of Burleson's son-in-law who took his meals with the Burlesons," according to an article in *Texas Monthly* magazine.

Brann leaped on the accusations of impropriety at the Baptist university to crow that no man was safe sending his daughter to the school and that it was good only for the manufacture of "ministers and Magdalenes," a

An undated early photo of the W.C. Brann monument in Oakwood Cemetery with the original "Truth" lamp intact. *Lee Lockwood Library and Museum.*

code word for prostitutes. Sufficient numbers of the Baylor student body were outraged enough to seize Brann from his office and drag him to campus—a noose around his neck—with the intention of lynching him for his attacks on the school, but the interference of faculty members stayed their hands. He signed, under duress, a retraction of his story and was allowed to return to his office; within days, he was printing anti-Baylor content the same as before.

By April 1, 1898, the rhetoric and vitriol had reached a fever pitch. Brann and his business editor were walking down Fourth Street toward a train station—he was purchasing tickets for his whole family to take a combined vacation and lecture tour that would take him away from the controversy he had caused for several weeks—when a man named Tom Davis emerged from his real estate office across the street and shot Brann in the back, "right where his suspenders crossed," according to several newspaper write-ups. Brann pulled his own gun and returned fire, hitting Davis multiple times. Both men died by the end of the next day.

Brann was laid to rest in a grave in Oakwood Cemetery surmounted by an elaborate headstone bearing only his monogram (WCB) on one side and a bas-relief image of his profile on the other. The top of the headstone was graced by a large Grecian lamp meant to signify the eternal flame of truth. At some point shortly after his burial, an unidentified person was alleged to have shot a pistol into the temple of Brann's graven image; it is true that the piece is damaged in this location, but impossible to know for sure its origins. (By 2009, the lamp had been stolen, and it remains missing as of this writing; it is theorized by some that it was stolen as part of a prank by a local fraternity or that it now resides at the bottom of the Brazos River, as noted in a *Texas Monthly* article.)

Despite Brann's widow's attempts to keep it alive, the *Iconoclast* died with its firebrand progenitor. But by 1911, the deadly edge of Brann's legacy had dulled sufficiently to entice Waco's Herz Brothers to print a two-volume set of Brann's writings, touted as a "suitable Christmas gift for father, husband, brother and friend" in an October 24 ad in the *Waco Morning News*. "We know of nothing more acceptable to people who are literarily inclined," the ad asserts. "Brann was an intellectual Titan. He had the philosophy of Carlyle, the brilliancy of Voltaire, the sarcasm of Desmoulins, the poetry of Ingersoll." Thus, Brann's life proved to be the inverse of a now-famous phrase from the 2008 movie *The Dark Knight*, "You either die a hero or live long enough to see yourself become the villain." Brann died a villain, but to some, at least, his poisoned pen and oft-brilliant mind were enough to earn him a seat at the antihero's banquet, even if it took a decade or more after his death to get there.

In 1912, the *Waco Morning News* ran a biography of Brann, and it included a good deal of editorializing on the style and legacy of his writing;

> *Mr. Brann has been classed as a humorist. This he was, and of a type peculiar to himself, but he was not content with merely having amused or entertained the people*[;] *he aspired to arouse public sentiment in the interest of certain reforms. He was a hater of shams and defied every form of fraud, hypocrisy and deceit. He made of his humor a whip with which to scourge from the temple of social purity every intruder there. He joined in no partisan schemes for place or power but, confident of his own ground, he would stand alone in the defiance of popular humbugs and frauds.*

Brann's writings would find favor among a strange mix of malcontents, philosophers, historians and—at least in one instance—Hollywood celebrities. A brief item in the September 11, 1929 *Waco News-Tribune* reports that its office received a "telegraphic request" from the Sells-Floto

The bas-relief image of Brann's profile, sporting purported bullet damage to the temple. *Author's collection.*

circus in Fort Worth to "have prepared upon the circus' arrival today a wreath which Tom Mix desires to place upon the grave of W.C. Brann, the Iconoclast….The circus management, in explaining the request, stated that the movie hero was a great admirer of the late Wacoan." How Mix, the "King of Cowboys" and star of almost three hundred movies, became a fan of Brann's is not noted, but the idea of a famous silent movie star paying tribute to Brann with a wreath laying ceremony is just the sort of seemingly incongruous combination one expects when Brann is concerned.

At least one local attempt was made to memorialize Brann's life as late as 1990: a one-man stage play called *O Dammit*, written by Jerry Flemmons and starring David Ellis, "invites the audience into the office of William Brann," according to a preview in the *Waco Citizen* of August 24 of that year. This homage to Brann puts him in a category with only one other nineteenth-century author to also inspire a one-man show about his life: Mark Twain, whose wit and wisdom were portrayed on stage by Hal Holbrook in *Mark Twain Tonight!* Not a bad legacy for a man considered so vile by some that he was shot in the back in broad daylight on a busy downtown street.

6

Telephus Telemachus Louis Augustus Albartus "Tel" Johnson and His Famous Tombs

What makes someone a local legend? Is it their contributions to a particular cause? An infamous mean streak, a genius for self-promotion or possessing vast quantities of wealth? Maybe it's their prowess at sports or their decades of public service through elected office? Or maybe it's the fact that after their death, there are immediate rumors that their final resting place inside a large mausoleum features them seated in a chair at a table, a glass of whiskey in one hand and a six-shooter in the other. In the case of the grandly named Telephus Telemachus Louis Augustus Albartus "Tel" Johnson, the circumstances of his burial—or, more accurately, burials—gave rise to an enduring piece of local lore that is repeated to this day.

Telephus Johnson was born in Alabama in 1822 to Hezekiah and Elizabeth Johnson. A *Waco News-Tribune* article by Marion Travis notes in a photo caption that Hezekiah was reportedly a "good-humored Methodist minister" who enjoyed giving his first children long "high-flown names." Tel married Mary Louisa Dunnica in 1844, and the Johnsons moved to Waco in 1852, when "Uncle Tel" was thirty years old. Within a decade of arriving in town, he had become one of its wealthiest citizens, amassing more than seven hundred acres of land, according to his entry in *The Handbook of Waco and McLennan County, Texas*. He was noted to be one of the "most remarkably unorthodox characters who ever lived here on the Brazos," according to a write-up in volume 50 of the *Southwestern Historical Quarterly*.

Johnson's landholdings included a parcel near Second Street, on which he built a large home for Mary and himself. (The cross-street was named Mary Avenue in her honor.) By all accounts, Tel was an active and highly visible member of the Waco community. In 1874, he was one of two bidders for the auctioning off of the "old courthouse," which he purchased with a winning bid of $575, according to a write-up in the May 25, 1924 issue of the *Waco News-Tribune*. (It is likely this purchase that led to his being "influential" in the location determined for that building's successor later that year.)

Tel Johnson died on January 27, 1875, at the age of fifty-two. Like most of his contemporaries, he was slated to be buried in First Street Cemetery; unlike many of them, he had the means to be laid to rest in a large, red brick mausoleum. Bearing four square columns and—based on the mounting hardware still evident on the outer walls—at least two large metal plaques on the exterior, the structure is one of the more imposing examples built in the cemetery. Perhaps owing to his flamboyant reputation, a rumor began almost immediately after the last brick was laid across the entryway that Tel was buried seated at a table, holding either one or all of the following: a pistol, a glass of whiskey or playing cards, depending on the teller.

Over time, the cemetery fell into a state of disrepair, and those with the means to do so began to relocate the remains of their antecedents to Oakwood Cemetery, a larger and better-maintained cemetery that opened in 1878. Johnson's family was among those who made the move, transferring his remains into a new aboveground crypt that was a considerable upgrade to the original brick mausoleum. A large white marble box topped with a plinth and bedecked in classical death-related imagery—including eight upside-down torches symbolizing a life extinguished by death—the crypt bears a large inscription above his name and birth and death dates: "Rest, Eternal Rest!"

Once Tel Johnson's body was relocated to his newest final resting place, it became easy to debunk the myth about the fanciful physical configuration of his much-talked-about mortal remains. And while no one has documented what they looked like when the original mausoleum was opened for the transfer, it is easy to note that the current crypt has no room for a skeleton to be seated at a table, with or without a sidearm.

An interesting side note about his widow, Mary Louisa. She married a man named John Tarleton, a local businessman, in 1876, a year after Tel's death. In a move unusual for the time, both parties had agreed to a prenuptial agreement based largely on Mary's large holdings left to her after Tel's death. Upon their marriage, Mary quickly learned that John owned

Telephus Johnson's crypt in Oakwood Cemetery. No guns, alcohol or gambling present, as far as we know. (This time.) *Author's collection.*

large tracts of land, thus greatly enhancing his perceived net worth. She was angry that despite his wealth, he was a "parsimonious" man who, to her mind, hoarded his money. Three years after their marriage, she filed for divorce, claiming that John had been violent toward her. A trial ended with no finding of violence on John's part, and both parties went their separate ways. Upon his death in 1895, John's assets and property were left to the founders of a college that was named in his honor: John Tarleton College (today, Tarleton State University).

II

A New Century

1

The Fabulous Hoffmannettes and *A Waco Romance*

A defining feature of the burgeoning middle class in early twentieth-century America was the ambition to provide the trappings of upper-class life despite lacking access to the generational wealth that made such activities possible for well-heeled families prior to the Industrial Revolution. Expanding access to a greater share of the wealth meant people who had previously struggled to survive were now thriving to the extent that they could begin to afford luxuries unheard of only a generation before. One of those luxuries was participation in the arts, and music instructors, art teachers and private tutors became more common as family incomes rose.

When it came to the world of dance in early 1900s Waco, two names stood out. Sisters Fay and Bird Hoffman made a reputation for themselves as the best-known purveyors of the terpsichorean muse, and their skill with a variety of steps influenced generations of Waco youngsters who hoped to follow in their graceful footsteps.

Fay (February 7, 1888–June 19, 1972) and Bird Hoffman (August 10, 1890–October 15, 1966) were born to a warm, loving, culturally focused family headed by W.H. Hoffman, an accountant with a history of service to the United States Post Office as a postmaster, and Ellie Draughon Hoffman, a "vibrant, gifted French" woman, according to Waco historian Roger Conger. He notes that the house was one of "love and mutual admiration, of mirth and gaiety, of the love of music, and art and dancing." The girls' love of dance was encouraged by their parents, and they began their training at a

Fay and Bird Hoffman, the "Fabulous Hoffmannettes," in an undated photo, probably circa 1920. *Lee Lockwood Library and Museum.*

young age. In 1908, they opened their own dance studio, which they would operate for the next fifty years.

The Hoffman sisters received their fair share of press coverage by the local media, such as a marvelously headlined piece in the October 5, 1919 issue of the *Waco News-Tribune*. Above a smiling photo of the sisters blared the all caps header: "SHIMMIE! NIX, SAY THESE," in what can only be described as the most 1919 headline about dance it is possible to imagine. The article goes on to report on the girls' recent trips to New York and Chicago and how they were bringing back new ideas about dance to their hometown:

> *Again do Misses Fay and Bird Hoffman make their bow to Waco dance fans after a successful season in the best salons de dance in New York and*

> *Chicago. During the summer months they ransacked the two metropoles in search of everything new and up-to-the-minute in dancing. Into the studios of Oscora Duyea, Vernonine Vestoy, Sonia Serova, Louis Chalif and others they dipped*[,] *tucking away into their nervous systems the rhythm and dearest dances for curly tops, sub-debs, eighteen-and-overs, and those who refuse to talk on the subject of years, which, of course, does not imply old age.*

An advertisement in the September 30, 1928 edition of the *Waco News-Tribune* gives details about the sisters' dance studio, which had grown to two locations by that point: one at Ninth and Franklin Avenues in the Maccabee Hall and a second in their home. The ad addresses "the Amateur, the Teacher, and the Professional" and points out the sisters' eleven years' study under instructors in New York and Paris. "Twenty-six teachers in Waco, and outlying towns, pupils of the Hoffmannettes," is also noted before adding, "Pupils of Hoffmannettes now playing in successful New York productions." Business on the eve of the Great Depression was good, and the sisters' reputation would allow them to continue their instruction for the next several decades, even as they grew into old age.

In 1973, a memorial was dedicated in Oakwood Cemetery to the memory of the Hoffmannettes. According to a May 2, 1973 article in the *Waco Tribune-Herald*, the memorial was sponsored by "Wacoans who had learned dancing and social graces from the Hoffman sisters." The inscription reads "The Hoffmannettes, Fay Hoffman–Bird Hoffman, Beloved Teachers of the Dance, 1908 to 1966." The ceremony was presided over by Roger Conger and Reverend Roy Sherrod of the First Presbyterian Church. Conger's eulogy was reproduced almost entirely in full in the article, and it gets to the heart of the two women and why they had such a lasting effect on generations of Wacoans:

> *When the two devoted sisters were born is of no consequence. They were born, less than three years apart, and they lived here more than four score years. Fully conscious of their beauty and their animation, they loved to dress alike and many persons mistook them for twins. They preferred dresses that were swirly, soft and diaphanous, and the haunting odor of spring violets hung about them like a lovely haze. They affected huge black beauty spots and wore their hair piled high in soft cascades. And as their years advanced, their light brown hair never turned to gray. It turned instead to an even more striking mahogany.*

> *Their gift for music and dancing had been apparent from an early age and they received from their doting parents the finest training the country could provide. By the year 1908, they had opened their own school of dancing and for over half a century hundreds of fortunate Waco girls, and a few Waco boys as well, shared the remarkable privilege of their teaching and unique personalities. The Hoffmannettes, as they were known from the first, were absolutely ageless. Children adored them and they in turn adored all children and lavished upon their pupils a bounty of encouragement, baby talk, affection diminutives and incomparable blithe spirit....*
>
> *Parents were enthusiastic over the hitherto hidden well-springs of grace and self-assurance the Hoffmannettes could so capably uncover and encourage in many a seemingly ungifted offspring. And as the years passed by, they broadened their curricula to include lessons for the more mature—ballroom dancing, calisthenics and physical culture.*
>
> *One of the great, sad lessons of history has been well described as "the terrible transitoriness* [sic] *of human accomplishment." The Misses Fay and Bird Hoffman are now gone to their heavenly reward. We know that wherever they are, there will be light and joy and beauty, and we their friends will not forget them but will cherish their memories like their own sweet violets.*

A curious episode in the lives of the Hoffman sisters took place in 1913. That's when the duo was featured in a motion picture filmed in Waco, fittingly titled *A Waco Romance*. The silent film was lost for decades until it was found in their former home—now the headquarters building for the Historic Waco Foundation, at 810 South Fourth Street—during a renovation. According to an article in the *Waco Tribune-Herald* published on March 16, 1975, the reel was delivered to Bill Cook, who was head of Baylor University's Drama Department. He held onto it for three years before "deciding to see how much of it could be salvaged." He obtained the assistance of longtime Waco congressman W.R. "Bob" Poage, and the film was transferred from its original 35mm glycerin format to modern, flame-proof 16mm by a firm in New Jersey. Of the original 800 feet of film, less than half—380 feet—could be salvaged.

Fortunately for history, the salvageable film featured a treasure-trove of footage of early twentieth-century Waco, including shots of the Amicable Building (the ALICO), the McLennan County Courthouse, Baylor

University, Cameron Park and the Washington Street "iron bridge." Unfortunately for viewers' sanity, the reconfigured footage was spliced together with no regard to the original narrative's internal logic, so scenes of young women on automobile rides with young men are interspersed with footage of a fire truck roaring down Austin Avenue or scenes of city leadership bowing to the camera in obviously staged settings with no bearing whatsoever on the *Waco Romance* storyline. As the *Tribune-Herald* article points out, "There is a semblance of a plot to the 'romance' but it appears that the usable parts of the film were not put back into proper sequence when it was reprocessed." Then, in an example of what today might be termed "throwing shade," writer Henry Beckham adds, "Cook, familiar with the involved plots of countless stage productions, claims to understand the story."

Attempting to make sense of the film is difficult, but the overall gist is one of a group of young women—two of whom are portrayed by Fay and Bird Hoffman, the other two by Ida Orand and Pauline Foster Stephens—falling into the company of two young men, played by A.C. McDavid and Will Burroughs. There is a car ride that departs from the front of Toby's Business College, with a stop at Sanger Brothers Department Store and then, ultimately, proceeds to Cameron Park. At some point during the ride, the two men are involved in a legal matter, as they are shown on the steps of the courthouse under the watchful eye of a man wearing a badge.

Back at Cameron Park, the car has broken down and will not start, so the four women and McDavid start walking. Eventually, they arrive at a bridge, and the women are picked up by a man in a wagon; McDavid is left to continue on foot, accompanied by a dog that has suddenly appeared. At some point, the Hoffman sisters are shown in flouncy dresses sitting in a tree, but they play no more part in the central storyline (such as it is). The final scene of *A Waco Romance* features a wedding (staged in front of a Methodist church but overseen by a man in full Episcopal priest attire) between a fifth girl (Grace Hawley) and Burroughs. Rice is thrown, additional random scenes of the Texas Cotton Palace are shown and the film comes to a confusing and abrupt end.

It is almost certain that *A Waco Romance* was a much more competently made and understandable affair when it was originally shot and edited in 1913. And it is tempting to be frustrated that so much of the original film was lost in the years the reel sat moldering in the Hoffman house attic. But ultimately, Waco historians are grateful that even this small amount of live footage of peak 1910s Waco exists today. And in 2017, the film footage—which is housed at Baylor's Texas Collection—was digitally restored by the Baylor Libraries' Digitization and Digital Preservation Services group, ensuring *A Waco Romance* will endure for generations to come. Perhaps one day some intrepid film buff will undertake a project to restore the footage to a semblance of order—an act of true love for anyone enamored with the story of Waco's past.

2

WACO'S PRIDE: HER FIRE DEPARTMENT

We take it for granted today, but the idea of an efficient, speedy, effective fire department was not the norm for many cities at the turn of the last century. And in a time of wooden structures, few working fire hydrants and a reliance on volunteer firefighters, the appearance of an uncontrolled fire within a city block could spell widespread disaster. As Waco grasped for even higher heights of modernity and prosperity in the new century, it made significant investments in a mechanized, professional fire department as a means of protecting significant investments in the city's economic and domestic infrastructure, creating a point of civic pride in the process. In 1902, a souvenir booklet of information about the fire department was issued as a special look back on the history and organization of a model firefighting company in early twentieth-century Texas.

The Waco Fire Department—in its professional organization—was established on April 23, 1873, a mere fourteen years after the official founding of the City of Waco in 1849. By 1902, the Waco Fire Department had become a regulated, professionally staffed and well-equipped outfit consisting of six companies with thirty-one paid firemen and hundreds of volunteers. In addition to four steamers, a hook and ladder (aerial) truck and four hose wagons, the department also boasted five thousand feet of hose and twenty-five horses. It also operated a Gamewell Electric Fire Alarm system that consisted of forty-eight street boxes and all accompanying apparatus to help locals spread an immediate alarm to the nearest fire station mere moments after a fire was spotted.

Firemen were on guard all hours of the day, with a night watch on duty from 9:00 p.m. to 6:00 a.m.; it required a time clock be punched every fifteen minutes to prove the men were active in their watch and not sleeping away the midnight hours on the city's dime. The souvenir booklet notes that the City of Waco—which owned all of the apparatus and paid firemen their salaries—allocated $1,700 per month for the maintenance of the department. "Out of this salaried men are paid, feed, repairs, horse shoeing and everything that is necessary to keep up the condition of the Department is paid out of this allowance," the booklet notes.

The overall effects of having a professional, fully-staffed fire department were spelled out in the final sentences of the booklet's opening pages: "The insurance of this city is rated as first-class. The percentage of losses are much less than any city of its size in the state. At all fires we have more volunteer firemen than is really necessary. These men are loyal to the city and its interest to their executive officers, and fight fires with more sincerity than regular paid men."

Perhaps one of the reasons these men were so much more "sincere" in their duties owes to the fact that there were specific guidelines spelled out for every class of fireman, from drivers to the night watch. A section of the booklet titled "House Rules for Paid Men" is instructive in this regard and worth reproducing here in its entirety as a way of helping modern readers understand just how well-disciplined and ahead of their time the men of the Waco Fire Department actually were.

> *Drivers: The drivers shall take proper care of their horses and apparatus; shall exercise the greatest caution in their keeping and management; shall keep their stables clean and harness in perfect order, and on no account leave their engine houses without leaving everything in readiness for immediate service.*
>
> *Engineers: Engineers of steamers shall be held responsible for the keeping of their engines in good and perfect order and ready at all times for immediate use; shall keep all parts of engine polished and clean, and should the driver be absent at the time of an alarm the engineer in charge shall drive the apparatus out.*
>
> *Chemical Engine: Engineer of Chemical Engine shall see that his engine is in good working order, and that at all times he has sufficient charges for immediate use, and that he shall keep all parts of engine clean and polished.*

Hook and Ladder Driver: Driver of Hook and Ladder Truck shall take proper care of his horses and apparatus; shall exercise the greatest caution in their keeping and management; shall keep the stable and harness clean and in perfect order; and see that everything belonging to said apparatus are in their proper place; also see when driving out that he has a proper tillerman with him.

Extra Men: It shall be the duty of extra men to assist the regular men in cleaning up when not on duty for regular men. They shall keep all extra horses and harness clean, horses fed and watered, and such other duties that may be assigned to them by custodians of engine house to which they belong.

Night Men: Night men must be at their respective stations at 9 o'clock p.m. sharp, and remain on duty until 6 a.m. They shall answer all fires and alarms same as regular paid men, help in placing the apparatus in proper place when returning from fires; also shall, when leaving engine house in morning, make up their beds and put their belongings in proper place.

Night Watch: Proper watch shall be kept at the different engine houses so that some of the permanent force shall always be on the lookout for fires. The custodian shall designate the watch; watch to begin at 12 a.m. and kept up until 6 a.m. They shall at all times be in the hearing of the telephones. Each man that is on watch must keep up the fires in heaters attached to engines all hours of the night. Should a fire be discovered out of their district, they must at once phone 166, stating the location of the fire as near as possible.

Cleaning Rooms: All paid members must take their turn in cleaning up the bedrooms and meeting hall; see that dirty clothes are kept in such places that the custodian may fix for them; see that bathroom and bathtub have their proper share and attention, and when any person uses the bathtub he must put same in clean and perfect order. (This means everybody.) Windows must be washed once a month, floors to be scrubbed once a week, yards as often as required.

Additional Rules: Spitting tobacco juice or other obnoxious stuff in and around the engine house is strictly forbidden. Loud and boisterous talking in and around the engine house will not be tolerated. Intoxicating liquors must not be kept or allowed to be drank in any part of the fire stations of this department, except by permission of the Chief. Paid members must not leave their respective stations without permission from the Chief or the executive officer in charge. This does not mean when going to meals.

In going to meals, at Central stations, only two will be allowed off at one time, other stations only one. Drivers, engineers, and extra men must have their work done by 9:30 a.m. at all stations, and then have themselves in proper uniform by 10 a.m., and should any visitor desire to see fire apparatus and horses, it shall be the duty of the paid men to show all courtesies due a visitor and a stranger. All paid men must not ask to get off oftener than is necessary. This getting off every few nights will not be entertained. Each man must remember that there are others who desire a leave of absence once in a while.

The Waco Fire Department Memorial in Oakwood Cemetery. *Author's collection.*

> *Should any of the above rules be violated by any paid man, he is subject to fifteen days lay off without pay, and second offence dismissed. This means every man that comes under "paid" department. The custodians of their respective stations shall see that these rules are strictly obeyed, and, if they find any rules being violated and same is not reported to the Chief, they themselves will be subject to fifteen days lay off without pay.*

With such an extensive set of expectations for its paid staff, it's easy to see why the department was held in such high esteem by turn-of-the-century Wacoans. So high was the regard for the city's firemen that the department was often referred to as the "Pride of the City of Waco," and the presence of a well-trained firefighting force was touted by local business owners and booster groups like the Young Men's Business League as evidence of the pro-business atmosphere present in Waco. Essentially, the message became a tacit promise: locate your business in Waco and our firefighters will ensure it is kept safe, a promise our competitors can't make.

The city's appreciation for its firefighting community was memorialized—literally—with an elaborate display in Oakwood Cemetery, erected in the 1880s. It features a tall pedestal topped with a statue of a firefighter holding a hose and standing next to a fire hydrant. Portions of the hydrant and the fireman's helmet are painted to give the granite monument a splash of color, and it is one of the more striking attractions in all of Oakwood. Funded by volunteer firefighters and committed to the memory of those who died in the line of service, it is a lasting tribute to the men who risked their lives to protect the lives and property of early twentieth-century Wacoans.

3

The YMBL, the Ad Club and Local Commerce

Hometown boosterism takes many forms: support of the high school sports team, shopping local, sporting the town's logo on your T-shirt. Professional boosterism in the case of early twentieth-century Waco can trace its roots back to the Young Men's Business League, a group of business professionals whose focus was to expand Waco's reputation and reach into the Central Texas region and beyond, with the hope of attracting new businesses, commercial firms and retailers to the city. Aiding in the quest to expose Waco's positive qualities to the world was the Waco Ad Club, which featured both male and female members and used many modern advertising tactics to promote the city at the regional, state and national level. This chapter will examine several photos of YMBL and Ad Club activities from the early twentieth century, both in Waco and on the road.

This group of Waco Ad Club women is posing on the steps of an unidentified building in front of a background featuring the group's logo and the phrase "Heart of Texas." The photo caption notes that the woman in the far back left is Florence Jeanette Boyd Gildersleeve, wife of Fred Gildersleeve (who took the photo), but the others are unidentified. The women are bedecked in promotional items bearing the Waco name, with a focus on the Texas Cotton Palace scheduled for October 31–November 15 of this undocumented year. (It is likely 1920, as the historical record indicates the Texas Cotton Palace took place during that date range only on this particular year.) In addition to Texas flags bearing the Cotton

A group of Waco Ad Club women pose in an undated photo; Mrs. Fred Gildersleeve at far left. *Lee Lockwood Library and Museum.*

Palace dates, several women are wearing sashes with the same information printed them, and others wear armbands emblazoned with the Waco name as well. It is likely this delegation—who were attending a tenth annual convention of some unknown group, based on the partially visible cover of a booklet held in the arms of the woman in the center—was chosen to represent the city of Waco to a larger body of Texans, and by the looks of their Waco paraphernalia and smiling faces, they appeared to have fully embraced the opportunity.

The YMBL loved trains. This is obvious to any researcher who spends time in the photographic archives available for perusal at several fine Waco institutions. This particular photo documents an "Ad Special"—a train chartered for a specific purpose, in this case, bringing George W. Coleman to Waco. Thanks to a surprising amount of documented detail, we know the photo was taken in 1911 while the train sat at rest at the Cotton Belt Depot (Fourth and Mary). Coleman is pictured at center (in the white suit and hat), and prominent Waco architect W.W. Larmour is pictured off to Coleman's left, also in a white suit, with his hat in his hand.

The most pertinent question to arise from this photo is "Who was George Coleman, and why did the YMBL bring him to Waco?" Thanks to

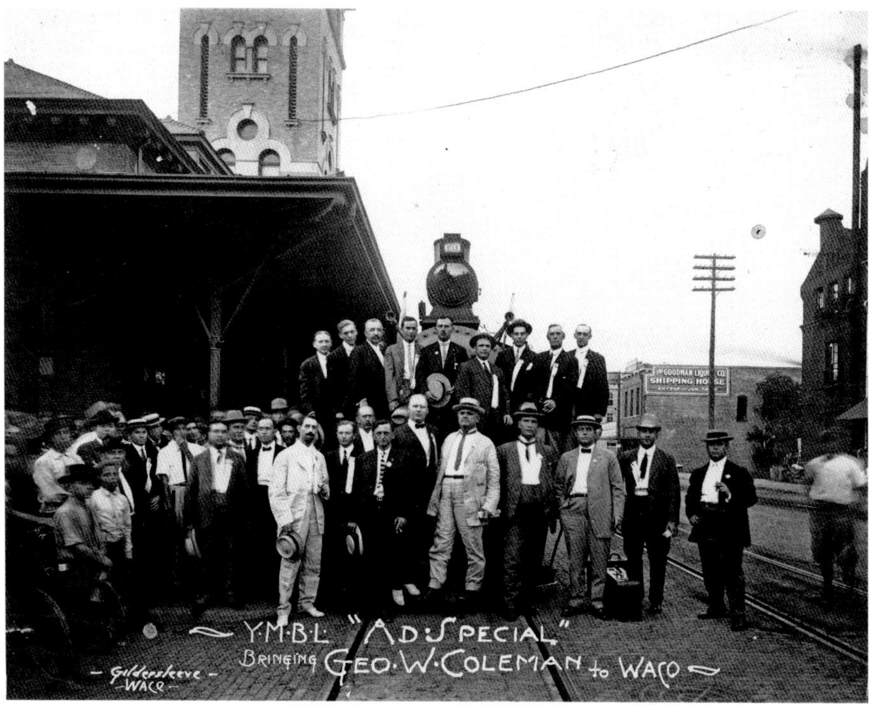

YMBL members pose with George Coleman and the "Ad Special" train that brought him to Waco. *Lee Lockwood Library and Museum.*

a November 1911 issue of *Texas Magazine*, we know that Coleman was the president of the Associated Advertising Clubs of America. Based in Boston, Coleman was a sought-after consultant on the ins and outs of advertising, and the City of Dallas enticed him to visit "in the interest of the 1912 convention," according to the *Texas Magazine* article. "President Coleman, for the national organization, conferred with the officers and executive committee of the Dallas Advertising League, and it was unanimously decided to hold the 1912 Convention [in Dallas] in May." The article goes on to reveal the reason for his appearance in Waco:

> *This was President Coleman's first visit to Texas, and if he ever entertained any doubt of Dallas' ability to properly take care of this great convention, it was soon dissipated. Dallas was a revelation to him, and I might add, so was each of the other Texas cities he visited. From Dallas he went to Fort Worth. Waco showed her enterprise by securing a special train to take him to that city. In turn he visited San Antonio, Houston and Galveston.*

> *At each city he was royally entertained and was given a sample of that true Southern hospitality which awaits those who attend the 1912 Convention. He left the State enthusiastic for Texas, and will sing her praises throughout the length and breadth of the land during the coming year.*

Chartering a special train to facilitate a visiting Bostonian's day trip to Waco was exactly the kind of over-the-top, specific and successful stunt that made the YMBL so successful in their promotional, fundraising and goodwill generating activities on behalf of Waco. But to really take his visit over the top (pardon the pun), the club staged a photo on the roof of the Amicable Building, which—as the caption on this photo notes—at twenty-two stories over downtown remains the city's tallest building. Gildersleeve added a punny title ("The Heighth [*sic*] of Advertising") to the photo, which features dozens of men crammed into the corner of the Amicable's roof for what would likely have been an impressive view from the top of the then only recently completed structure.

YMBL members pose with George Coleman atop the Amicable (ALICO) building. *Lee Lockwood Library and Museum.*

Groundbreaking ceremony for a new "white way" lights system, presided over by YMBL. *Lee Lockwood Library and Museum.*

Another favorite pastime of the YMBL was staging publicity photos that coincided with public improvements. This 1915 photos shows members of the group at the corner of Third Street and Austin Avenue. The occasion is the ceremonial groundbreaking—literally—for a new system of "white way" lights that would be installed down Austin. This particular corner would have been at the corner of the public square and Austin, an important crossroads and the beginning of the avenue's long march through downtown Waco.

4
Fred Gildersleeve's Eye for Waco

Few professions have had as significant an effect on modern historians as that of the commercial photographer of the 1880s–1950s. Their eye for documenting the businesses, activities, daily lives and newsworthy events of their hometowns provide today's researchers with invaluable records of life in the past. And in the case of Waco's historic photographic record, no one equals the output of Fred A. Gildersleeve.

Even the most casual fan of Waco history has likely seen evidence of Gildersleeve—or "Gildy," as he was often known—and his legacy. A quick glance into the corner of any one of hundreds of photos taken in Waco between 1905 and 1958 will reveal the telltale signature: Gildersleeve-Waco. Gildersleeve was, in every sense of the word, a pioneer of the photographic art: daring, innovative, fearless and, above all, proficient. For half a century, he could be seen all over Waco with his box camera in tow, taking pictures of social gatherings and business meetings, car crashes and school events, football teams and public ceremonies. It seemed like nothing happened under the Waco sky that escaped his omnipresent camera.

Gildersleeve was born in 1880, the son of a Civil War veteran who died young, at the age of forty-six, in 1881. The family moved to Missouri, where he finished school and dabbled as a horse jockey, a pursuit that was aided by his diminutive stature. In 1898, Gildy was gifted his first camera, an 1898 Kodak box model, given to him by his mother. After studying photography at the Illinois College of Photography, Gildersleeve moved to Waco in 1905 to pursue his career as a professional photographer. His sister moved to Waco at about this same time to open an osteopathic medicine practice; their mother eventually moved to Waco and lived with Gildy's sister. Gildy married Florence Boyd in 1908 and lived in a home next door to his sister on Ethel Avenue.

Roger Conger, in a piece he wrote for the Winter 1976 issue of *Waco Heritage & History*, said that Gildersleeve's arrival in Waco meant he was "at the right place at the right time. It was good luck all around. The little city was blessed with an absolute abundance of civic and commercial talent and enterprise—men who were going places. And they carried Waco—and Gildersleeve—with them." Conger is absolutely correct in his assessment that both the city of Waco and Gildersleeve experienced an amazing period of growth and prosperity coincident with each other. In a sense, Waco's growing prosperity fueled Gildy's own upward rise, and as a way of giving back, he poured himself into civic pursuits at an almost inconceivable level. According to his entry on the Waco History website, the Standard Blue Book of Texas (1920 edition) lists him as "a member of the Masons, York Rite, Shriners, Rotary Club, Ad Club, Young Men's Business League, Chamber of Commerce and serving on committees of Liberty Loan, the Salvation Army and the Red Cross." With that kind of public involvement, Gildy would have been among Waco's movers and shakers all year round.

It was fortunate that Gildersleeve chose Waco as his final hometown, because the period in which he operated his photography studio saw several major transitional events: World War I, the Roaring Twenties, the Great Depression, World War II and the postwar boom, to name a few. And he began to make a name for himself early on, first by documenting the construction of the Amicable Life Insurance Company building (now known as the ALICO), then for photographing a massive outdoor banquet in 1911—dubbed the "Prosperity Banquet"—where he rigged a series of flash charges to go off at the same time, exposing hundreds of revelers seated at tables set up on downtown city streets in what would become one of his most famous photographic achievements. In 1913, he created what was at the time the largest reproduction of a photograph on record: a ten-foot-wide print of the Texas Cotton Palace that required special paper to be delivered to him by the Eastman Kodak Company just to get it printed. The fame he gained from this achievement helped spur him to greater prominence on the local—and now, national—photography scene.

It was the advent of World War I that gave him another of his claims to fame in the form of aerial photography. Thanks to the establishment of Rich Field by the U.S. Army Air Service in 1917, a steady stream of biplanes circled the skies around Waco as pilots trained to fly combat and surveillance missions over the battlefields of Europe. Gildy was "immediately upon an intimate, elbow-bending basis with the commanders" at Rich Field, as Conger put it, and he began charming his way onto sorties being flown around the Waco area. Hauling his trusty camera and tripod along with him into the second seat of a military aircraft, Gildy snapped some of the earliest aerial photographs in the state, including those of downtown Waco, the Amicable building and the earliest known aerial photos of Baylor University.

Likely due to his earlier affinity for horse racing, Gildy was an inveterate lover of sports of all kinds, particularly fishing, which he documented in photos during trips to Mexico and the Gulf coast of Texas. He was the official photographer of Baylor football from 1909 through the mid-1950s, and his group photos of those early twentieth-century Baylor Bears teams provide some of the best photographic evidence of the evolution of the sport at the collegiate level in Texas.

Gildersleeve's adherence to the old ways showed through in an anecdote related in a 1961 write-up in the *Waco Tribune-Herald*. An unnamed *News-Tribune* city editor asked Gildy to take a photo of a group of National Guardsmen in front of the armory building at Twelfth and Washington. Gildy agreed, but due to his refusal to use "speed cameras," he insisted that the men had to stand perfectly still during the shoot.

> *So the city editor got the guardsmen to pose with their legs stuck out in front of them as if they were marching, and hold it like that while Gildersleeve squeezed the bulb. Well, you can imagine what the picture looked like. Not like marching men. It looked, curiously enough, like a lot of men standing still, each with one leg stuck out in front of them. Thereafter the city editor was content with Gildersleeve pictures as was. No action.*

While Gildy's life seemed to be one of a constant upward trajectory for several decades, it would all begin to come back down to earth beginning around 1943, when he and his wife of thirty-five years ended their marriage in divorce. At the same time his marriage was dissolving, a large collection of hundreds of negatives captured on acetate film were destroyed in a fire in a dumpster. His older glass-plate negatives were spared, and many were stored in a shed in the backyard of his house, where they sat for many years until Roger Conger convinced him to let him evaluate their condition. Conger related,

> *Finally one day, to my surprise, he acceded, saying, "Aw, heck, come on."… When the musty door was drawn open the sight which greeted us was sickening.*
>
> *The accumulated weight of the dozens of flat cartons of heavy glass, stored in a section of too-light wood shelving, had literally pulled the shelves loose, perhaps years before, and allowed the entire treasure to crash forward across the floor. There they lay in a shattered pile, with half of more effectually lost and destroyed. I can recollect that Gildy stood there at the door, staring in stunned silence, for several seconds. His reaction then would have to be described as a highly pungent outburst.*

Conger convinced Gildersleeve to let him clean up the mess and salvage the plates that were the least damaged. This ended up being more than one thousand plates, which Conger eventually donated to The Texas Collection at Baylor University, where they remain to this day. In 2019, interim dean of Baylor Libraries John S. Wilson and audio/visual curator Geoff Hunt published a book of Gildersleeve's prints titled *Gildersleeve: Waco's Photographer*. Many of the photos in that work were derived from the glass-plate negatives saved by Conger in the late 1950s.

Gildersleeve died on February 26, 1958, of pneumonia complicated by atherosclerosis. He preceded his former wife in death by seven years, and the two never reconciled after their acrimonious divorce. They had no children, but Gildy's legacy to the people of Waco proved to be priceless in the form of his tireless documentation of Waco life for the better part of half a century. This chapter closes out with a few of his lesser-known photos that attempt to illustrate just a taste of the range of subjects Gildy captured as the "Mathew Brady of Waco."

This undated photo of a Salvation Army Christmas celebration bears many of the hallmarks of the Gildersleeve style. The main focal point of the action, a group arranged on a section of lawn on the city square, features people standing stock still and looking directly at the camera, a necessity to keep their faces in focus. Several blurs around the perimeter of the shot indicate motion unaccounted for on Gildy's part, including a buggy or automobile in the background and a person walking in the left middle distance near the area of damage to the original print. But the quality of

Results of a Salvation Army Christmas drive arranged on town square. *Lee Lockwood Library and Museum.*

Gildersleeve's lens and camera gives the photo extremely good detail and allows modern viewers to pick out small details like the names written on the sides of buggies in the background or the labels of donated foodstuffs in baskets on the ground.

Swimmers enjoy a dip in the Natatorium pool in the top photo on page 72. While keeping the group of aquatic enthusiasts completely still is out of the question, Gildy does a good job of framing up a large group of people in a cavernous indoor space. Once again, his high-quality equipment allows for examination of small details, in particular the signs posted around the pool bearing warnings like, "Bathers must take a shower bath before entering pool," and "Wrestling or running positively forbidden."

This bottom image, taken on April 16, 1951, shows the aftermath of a truck crash into the front of the Shade Shop, located at Eleventh and Washington Avenues. This photo represents another of his areas of subject matter, that of the newsworthy event or unusual crowd-drawing opportunity.

Swimmers enjoy the indoor pool at the Natatorium Hotel, circa 1920s. *Lee Lockwood Library and Museum.*

Aftermath of a semi truck colliding with the Shade Shop, April 16, 1951. *Lee Lockwood Library and Museum.*

Main gates of the Cotton Palace grounds, undated. *Lee Lockwood Library and Museum.*

It is framed in a way to capture both the main subject of the action but also almost a dozen bystanders in various states of gawking at the scene.

The main gates of the Cotton Palace grounds are pictured here in this undated photo. The facility, located at Thirteenth and Clay, operated from 1910 to 1930 and was home to an annual celebration of all things cotton and agriculture. While the grounds drew the most praise for its main exhibition building—another of Gildersleeve's favorite subjects—he also captured its more utilitarian areas, like these turnstiles and ticket window. It was his attention to capturing even the least flashy of subjects that makes his work invaluable to today's Waco historians.

5

Images of Working-Class Waco

The stories of working-class people rarely grab the headlines of a historical retrospective. Authors and historians tend to focus on the big names, the major stories, the tragedies and the once-in-a-lifetime events to give their narratives momentum and interest. But one thing that makes Waco unique is that over the course of its history, a number of excellent photographers made the documentation of the city's working class a part of their daily work, and we are fortunate to have hundreds of pictures of men and women—and sometimes children—caught in the midst of their workaday routines. And while we may not have the full story behind why each moment was committed to film, it is worth taking time here to look at and appreciate some of the unique examples of the past of working-class Waco available to us today.

The top image on the facing page is an interior view of the Sanger Brothers offices, labeled as being taken on September 15, 1919, which is odd, because the calendar on the back wall clearly shows the date as Monday, September 8. But as the 15 of September also fell on a Monday in 1919, it is reasonable to assume that the date of the photo was actually the date it was developed and printed, and photographer Fred Gildersleeve simply mislabeled it. Regardless, it is a fascinating look at a back-of-the-house operation for one of Waco's largest retailers. A fleet of secretaries and operators is arranged in the room, almost entirely female. In fact, of twenty people captured in the image, only five are men, reflecting a new reality in the American workforce as World War I came to an end and women's roles outside the home were becoming more prominent.

Staff of the Sanger Brothers Department Store, probably 1919. *Lee Lockwood Library and Museum.*

The "Working Boys" Club pose with pigs and parcels on the Waco Square, circa 1920. *Lee Lockwood Library and Museum.*

Members of the "Working Boys Club" pose with their porcine companions in the bottom photo on the previous page. The magnificent Waco City Hall is visible in the background, and in the midground is a wagon laden with bales of hay; on the ground in the foreground are boxes whose labels indicate they contain merchandise destined for the shelves of the Sanger Brothers store. The men and boys assembled on and nearby the wagon appear to be an assortment of young boys and men in work day attire, including overalls, caps and weather-beaten hats.

Two women pose in front of the Purple Cow Sandwich Shop, located on the ground floor of the Raleigh Hotel. According to an article on the Louis Grell Foundation website, the Purple Cow name was given to a series of cafés and coffee shops located in hotels operated by the Albert Pick company, a chain to which Waco's Raleigh belonged at the time. The purple cow in question was the subject of a poem published in 1895, and the Pick company asked Grell to paint a series of murals (in a cartoon style) of the cow as part of the décor for the restaurants.

Employees of the Purple Cow Sandwich Shop standing outside the Raleigh Hotel, where the café was located, circa 1942. *Lee Lockwood Library and Museum.*

The Waco location of the Purple Cow featured an unknown number of Grell's murals in its décor.

Though the image below is technically of a lignite mine in Rockdale—about an hour south of Waco—it is notable both because it captures the gritty realities of working men in a dangerous industry and because it features Waco's own photographic man-about-town, Fred Gildersleeve (holding shovel at far right). Gildy's visit to the facility is shrouded in unknowns: was he hired to document the work there? Was he on a goodwill mission on behalf of a group like the Waco Ad Club or the Young Men's Business League? Or did he simply have an interest in documenting the backbreaking labor of an important industry? The reasons for his visit are unclear, but this photo is evidence of his interest in making sure all kinds of workers found their way in front of his lenses.

Staff of the women's shoes section of the Goldstein-Migel department store are shown in the undated photo on the next page. Goldstein-Migel was one of Waco's most esteemed retailers, with roots dating back to the

Lignite miners pose with Fred Gildersleeve outside a mineshaft, circa 1920. *Lee Lockwood Library and Museum.*

Interior view of Goldstein-Migel women's shoes department, undated. *Lee Lockwood Library and Museum.*

nineteenth century. The store worked to stay on the leading edge of business innovations, including being among the first to install air conditioning and public restrooms. The location seen here is the original downtown location; a second location at the Lake Air Mall opened in the 1960s in an effort to cater to people moving to Waco's suburbs. By 1984, both locations had closed.

6

"The Church That Was Built in a Day"

Although the building was never meant to stand the test of time, and the finished product was small and modest compared to other, better-known examples in town, the story of how a group of people got together to build a church over the course of a single day is one of Waco's unique hidden gems, and luckily for us, it was caught on film by Waco photographer Fred Gildersleeve.

The structure in question was to be formally named the Herring Avenue Methodist Church, but it quickly became known as the "church built in a day." The audacious plan to build a functioning church house in a single day took root under the pastoral direction of Reverend H.L. Munger, who enlisted work supervisor Oscar Myre (a name that is neither a typo nor a made-up name) to oversee construction. A 1915 article in the *Waco Morning News* notes that "the foundations were laid in the morning, and by night it had been built, the windows and doors put in, the roof on, floors laid, and a coat of paint put on. Services were held that night."

This print shows four of Gildersleeve's photos from that day, incorrectly labeled January 11, 1911. (The construction actually took place on January 12.) In the upper left, work crews can be seen posing with lumber and framing elements at 8:05 a.m. Some site preparation has already taken place, with concrete footings arranged along the ground that would support the foundation of the modest building. A 1961 article in the *Waco Citizen* notes that the dimensions of the building would be thirty feet by sixty feet. On the horizon in the background of the photo is the main building of the Methodist Children's Home.

Four images of the "church they built in a day," Herring Avenue Methodist Church, January 12, 1911. *Lee Lockwood Library and Museum.*

By noon, a great deal of work had already been accomplished. The building's walls were complete, and a portion of the roof had been framed toward the rear of the structure. Nearly a dozen men can be seen swarming the nascent house of worship, applying wooden siding, roof panels and other necessary structural elements.

At bottom left we are given a view of the finished interior of the church, which features electric lighting and a handsome prefabricated altarpiece on the far wall. A carpet—possibly made of painted canvas for durability—lines the main aisle, and the open windows are set in walls sporting a fresh coat of paint. Also notable is the inscription stamped on the back of the temporary chairs arranged in the sanctuary: R.T. Dennis & Co. The R.T. Dennis Company was one of Waco's largest retailers, sporting an enormous location downtown that carried household goods, furniture, silverware and all manner of consumer goods. (It would be destroyed with great loss of life in the 1953 Waco Tornado that pulverized large swaths of downtown, ultimately killing 114 people.)

Finally, a finished view of the structure's exterior is provided at lower right. The layout is of a neat, trim rectangle with an extended front entry atop four short steps. Though bare of ornamentation, it does feature some fine exposed rafters and gleams with a fresh coat of paint, making it an attractive structure, especially considering the speedy nature of its erection.

The *Morning News* article of 1915 points out that in just four years' time, the "church has since been remodeled and enlarged, and is now quite commodious. Rev. R.F. Brown, the pastor, is a worthy successor of the live wire conditions which initiated the church and there is now a membership of 350." In 1961, a *Waco Citizen* article noted that about ten members who were originally part of the congregation in 1911 still survived, and the building's fiftieth anniversary "golden celebration" would feature a number of those survivors.

While the original "church built in a day" building was never meant to stand the test of time, the Herring Avenue Methodist Church survived for decades, adding a much larger brick sanctuary on the site at 1302 Herring just a few short years after the original frame building sprang up. Eventually, the church dissolved and its congregants joined other United Methodist churches in the area. But the people with ties to the "church they built in a day" will always have a claim to something special about their small but mighty church and the faithful place it occupies in the history of Waco.

III

Tales of War and Violence: World War I and the Interwar Years

1

The "Little Rough Riders"

With today's proliferation of opinions and options when it comes to the subject of how to raise kids, it can often be jarring to look back and see what activities the children of yesteryear undertook in their spare time. In early twentieth-century Waco, before the rise of television, the internet and complex questions about how much a child's future is dependent on their preadolescent identities, kids were often left to their own devices in the hours between sleep and school. That could mean time spent carrying out household chores or preparing for a future vocation or, in the case of a squad of Waco boys, forming a quasi-paramilitary group dubbed by locals as the "Little Rough Riders."

From a report written by Mary Edmond Lindsey and reproduced in the Winter 1979 issue of *Waco Heritage & History*, we learn a great deal about the activities of a group of boys ages six to twelve who were caught up in the fervor surrounding the exploits of the real Rough Riders, the common nickname for the First United States Volunteer Cavalry. Raised in 1898 in response to the sinking of the USS *Maine* and destined for fame under their commander, Colonel Theodore Roosevelt, the Rough Riders were among the most famous soldiers of the era thanks to Roosevelt's having written a history of the regiment and their later appearances in Hollywood movies based on their adventures.

Lindsey's write-up notes that the Little Rough Riders were informally begun sometime around 1898 and persisted into the new century; their genesis is given as "the aftermath of an entertainment given by Miss Emma

Beer and Mrs. W.H. Hoffman in which there was a company of small boys called the Roosevelt Rough Riders." (Close readers from the entry on Fay and Bird Hoffman will recognize their father's name in the preceding sentence.) The boys' appearance was apparently quite impressive, with "uniforms…of khaki with belt and brass buckles and buttons, a large military hat and leggings."

The company was quite large, numbering more than two dozen, including their "captain," Leslie Gardner, and "first lieutenant" Harry Hoffman, with "first sergeant" George Novich representing the noncommissioned officer class. The boys would routinely gather to hone their marching and drilling skills; at times, they participated in "sham battles" and overall were "much feted and admired." Such was their status that they began to be called on to participate in receptions for visiting dignitaries. When Spanish-American veterans returned to Waco at the end of that conflict, an "interesting program" had been arranged to welcome them; among the entertainment was an appearance by the Little Rough Riders. They repeated this service at local events for William Jennings Bryan (1899) and Admiral Winfield Scott Schley, the hero of the Battle of Santiago de Cuba during the Spanish-American War.

The company's presence in town was apparently one that generated a great deal of enjoyment among Waco's adult population. From Lindsey's report:

> *On the beautiful Gardner lawn a flag was presented to the company with suitable ceremonies, followed by cake and ice cream and boyish play. Socially they were the lions and scarcely a week passed that they were not entertained by some admiring friend or mother. Mr. Ramsey Cox carried them by train to Fowler for a wonderful camp. The Little Rough Riders drilled and romped on Mrs. J.C. Dean's beautiful lawn on Wednesday afternoons and when they were tired of play they took up a line of march toward the north and landed at a soda fountain counter downtown where they proceeded to refresh their infant stomachs with "Step It Babe" and Dewey mixtures in true military style. Mrs. Novich, Mrs. Symes, Mrs. Gardner, and others entertained them with lawn parties and the always acceptable ice cream and cake.*

Despite best efforts to the contrary, time did not stand still for the boys of the Little Rough Riders, and the realities of an interconnected and rapidly modernizing world soon caught up to them in the form of America's entry into World War I in 1917. And for two of their number, they would find their final rest on the battlefields of Europe. James A. Edmond (noted as "the little six year old Rough Rider" by Lindsey) and Jack Parnum were both killed in action in France. Parnum, a native of Glasgow, Scotland, had been a musician at the Hippodrome Theatre and an organist at Waco's First Presbyterian Church before he joined the U.S. Army. He died of wounds sustained while fighting in France on April 26, 1918, and was buried at the Lijssenthoek Military Cemetery in Poperinge, Belgium.

A minute book from the First Presbyterian Church provides a short write-up and reflection on Parnum and his importance to Waco:

> *In memory, John Wescomb Parnum, aged 30 years, organist in this church, on leave of absence, fell on the field of battle in France, May 1918.* [Author note: this incorrect date is due likely to the slow speed at which information on killed and wounded service members reached the States from Europe's battlefields.] *These words are brief and blunt with paint. They explain the little service flag on the organ.*
>
> *We would not think that Jack would not return. He resigned his place but was granted leave of absence instead. His heart's desire was to return, if it could be, to this organ and choir. But he has passed into the realm of eternal praise and glory. As Pastor, Officers Choir and congregation of the First Presbyterian Church we wish to bear testimony to the wonderful grace of his character. He never gave nor took offense; he was always most gentle, courteous and patient. His cheer and perseverance were abounding and his tone was pure and pleasant.*
>
> *We thank God for him. We share the pain of his loss with his mother, brother and young wife. He was ours too. The first of our number to fall on the battlefield, our hearts thrill with emotion that he gave us his own life for God and for us.*

Parnum's sacrifice in blood-soaked France pays tribute to the high ideals that he embodied in his life, and it is easy to see how some of his noble traits could be traced back to his days "playing soldier" in the Little Rough Riders. Waco has sent its sons off to fight in conflicts dating back to the American Civil War, and Parnum would not be the first—or the last—to be denied a chance to return to the scene of his boyhood, idyllic and joyful as it had been.

2

Waco's Refined Presence on a Merciless Dreadnought

Carl von Clausewitz famously stated in his book *On War*—published posthumously by his widow in 1832—that "war is simply a continuation of politics by other means." This dictum proved to be one of his most famous insights into the nature of armed conflict, and it is a nice springboard into a story about local Waco politics and their manifestation in the form of a silver service installed aboard the USS *Texas*, a New York–class battleship and the only surviving World War I dreadnought left in America.

The USS *Texas* was commissioned on March 12, 1914, and would go on to serve admirably in both World War I and World War II. It was a modern ship in every sense of the word and was reportedly the first to feature antiaircraft guns and the first to direct where its guns should fire using firing directors and rangefinders, a precursor to using computers to accomplish these tasks. Over the course of the two world conflicts, *Texas* earned numerous distinctions, including five battle stars for the five campaigns in which it participated during World War II.

Prior to *Texas*'s service in World War I, the ship participated in an action that would be labeled the "Tampico Incident," involving the detaining by Mexican troops of an American gunboat at the Mexican city of Tampico. The *Texas* was sent to the waters off Veracruz in a show of force meant to suppress any ideas on the Mexicans' part of engaging in further armed conflict with the United States. The display worked, and the *Texas* entered into a regular service rotation near the Mexican coast until November 1914, when it steamed for Galveston.

It was at Galveston during this refitting that Waco's Young Men's Business League (YMBL) comes into play. It was customary for all battleships to be gifted a set of silver serving utensils, given to the ship by the citizens of the state for which it was named. According to an article in *Texas Monthly* magazine, the *Texas* already had one 1895 service from the original USS *Texas*, but a new set was required for the ship commissioned in 1914. A statewide fundraising effort was undertaken to raise the $10,000 needed to commission and purchase the silver set. Although donations came in from all over Texas, it was the YMBL's $1,600 that was the single largest contribution to the Gorham Silver Company, which produced the twenty-eight-piece set.

According to the *Texas Monthly* article, the set included

> *an epergne* [an ornamental centerpiece]*; two electrified candelabras; coffee, tea, and chocolate services with sugar bowls and creamers; water pitchers; and serving trays, all in the popular Mission style and all adorned with some kind of visual reference to the state of Texas, usually the Lone Star or a cluster of cotton bolls. The most imposing piece was a twelve-gallon punchbowl with cups and a ladle.*

The complete silver service commissioned for the USS *Texas*. *Lee Lockwood Library and Museum.*

Dignitaries assembled on the deck of the USS *Texas* for a ceremony dedicating the ship's silver service, November 7, 1914. *Lee Lockwood Library and Museum.*

The punchbowl is often cited as the most interesting piece due to its handles, which are ornamental figures of Stephen F. Austin and Sam Houston. One side of the bowl is engraved with an image of the Texas capitol building, above which is a likeness of Governor Oscar Branch Colquitt. But the reverse side is of importance to Waco, as it features an engraving of the YMBL building in Waco, a nod to the group's importance in raising the needed funds to acquire the service.

On November 7, 1914, a ceremony was held on the deck of the *Texas* to present the silver service to the ship's commander, Captain Albert Grant. The entire service was laid out on tables set up behind one of the *Texas*'s massive fourteen-inch guns, the punchbowl on its custom stand taking center stage. In a Fred Gildersleeve photo of the ceremony, the side of the punchbowl featuring the YMBL building is visible.

Any Wacoans concerned that their hard-raised funds would go toward anything considered an intoxicant could rest easy: the *Texas Monthly* article notes that because the secretary of the navy in 1914, Josephus Daniels, was a strict prohibitionist, "nothing stronger than grape juice was ever served from this magnificent punchbowl," as Daniels had declared that all U.S. naval vessels would be dry.

3

The Hanging of Roy Mitchell

Likely the Last Public Execution in Texas

Waco's history with racially motivated extralegal executions—more commonly known as lynchings—is well-documented and a dark spot on the city's past. The most infamous example is the 1916 lynching of Jesse Washington, an event so bloody and heinous it earned the nickname the "Waco Horror." And while Waco was not unique among southern cities as a haven for people in authority harboring racial animus toward African Americans, it had earned a reputation for mob violence in the eyes of the American public that—correctly or incorrectly—persisted for decades. This perception was certainly in place during a series of events leading up to the public execution of a black man named Roy Mitchell in 1923. While Mitchell's hanging was considered a legal execution, and it was a far cry from the mob lynching of Jesse Washington, the events leading up to Mitchell's execution were replete with many of the racially motivated and stomach-churning details all too common to stories from its era.

According to a write-up on the Mitchell case in Michael Newton's *Hunting Humans: An Encyclopedia of Modern Serial Killers*, the grisly affair started with a single murder on May 7, 1922. That's when someone used an axe to murder William Driskell, who served as a deputy constable for Waco. Driskell's pistol and some personal effects were stolen, and police had no leads. Just over two weeks later, on May 25, the killer struck again: he shot and killed twenty-one-year-old Harvey Bolton, who was parked in a car with his girlfriend outside of Waco. The woman was raped by the killer but left alive. The victim accused a man named Jesse Thomas as her attacker. Thomas was shot to death by the girl's father and his body burned by a lynch mob. For the moment, it was believed that justice had been done and that the killings would come to an end.

That notion was laid to rest when another couple, parked near Lover's Leap in Cameron Park, were attacked by a black man with a shotgun. The male, Grady Skipworth, was killed instantly by a blast to the head; the woman, Naomi Boucher, was thrown over the cliff but survived because a tree broke her fall. According to Newton's write-up, "Once more, an innocent black [man] was accused, but Waco had learned its lesson. An all-white jury acquitted the suspect, despite Boucher's identification, and he was released in a storm of applause from the court."

By late 1922, it was obvious that the string of murders—three white men, all shot to death by a black man—was likely tied together, and Waco citizens were gripped by fear of a serial killer lurking in their midst. Racial tensions were already high on the heels of the Jesse Washington lynching just six years earlier, and the rise in Ku Klux Klan activity in Waco certainly contributed to a toxic atmosphere around town. On January 10, 1923, a "black gunman leaped onto the running board of a car passing through Cameron park, jabbing a shotgun through the passenger's window, but he was knocked to the ground without firing a shot," according to Newton. "He left behind a checkered cap, delivered to police as evidence, but nearly three weeks would elapse before its owner was identified."

On January 20, two more murders were carried out. The modus operandi was similar to past attacks: a young couple, W.E. Holt and Ethel Denecamp, was parked outside the Waco city limits in a car when a man jumped out of the shadows and shot Holt to death before beating Denecamp to death and fleeing into the night in the couple's stolen car. The car would prove to be a key break in the case, as it was discovered on a city street the next day, where the killer had abandoned it. At the same time, a man named Jesse Wedlow told authorities that the checkered cap they had recovered on January 10 belonged to a Louisiana man named Roy Mitchell, who had been in Waco for some time.

It is worth pausing here to consider the circumstances under which the majority of these attacks took place. With the exception of the first murder—that of Driskell, who was in his garage at home—the attacks took place in remote areas outside the Waco city limits, including inside Cameron Park. The park is one of Waco's most beautiful natural features, a massive urban park surrounded today by the Brazos River and a large part of the older neighborhoods of Waco. It was then (and remains now) largely undeveloped and wild, with several miles of paved roads but many more acres of trees, heights, trails and remote areas perfect for lovesick teenagers and homicidal maniacs alike to find seclusion for their activities of choice.

Also noteworthy is the role of the automobile in all but the first assault. As more and more Americans were investing their pre-Depression dollars in automobiles in the 1920s, they found with their purchase an expanded sense of freedom, an opportunity to go beyond the usual radius of their daily lives and into unexplored territory, even if that just meant traveling five miles outside of town to spend some alone time with one's romantic partner. That newfound freedom often came with a price, though, as joyriding young people could be lured by the thrill of easy speed into believing they were invincible, beyond the reach of local authorities and able to outrun any potential threat. This could lead to a lowering of the guard, a lack of spatial awareness and a perfect opportunity for someone intent on doing them harm to carry out a dastardly attack.

Police arrested Mitchell on a gambling charge on January 30, ten days after the murders of Holt and Denecamp. A search of his home turned up property stolen from murder victim Skipworth, as well as Driskell's handgun and holster. Mitchell was taken to jail, and after three days he confessed to five murders: those of Driskell, Bolton, Skipworth, Holt and Denecamp. Mitchell was brought to trial twice in March, but not before recanting his confession and claiming he had only confessed because of fear he would be tortured or lynched if he did not. According to Patricia Bernstein's book *The First Waco Horror*, Mitchell's wife, Minnie, and his ten-year-old daughter, Marguerite, were present at both trials and testified that Mitchell had been at home at the times of the killings. After deliberations that lasted "minutes," Mitchell was found guilty on all counts and sentenced to die by hanging.

At this point in the story, it is reasonable to fear that Mitchell's execution would be carried out not by a duly certified agent of the state but at the hands of thousands of angry townspeople gathered outside the courthouse, rope in hand and looking for immediate vengeance. And in the case of Jesse Washington, that is indeed what had happened. But despite the rising levels of KKK influence on city politics, and the past track record of Waco's responses to similar cases, the end of Roy Mitchell came after a concerted effort on the part of public officials, including the mayor and sheriff, to subdue threats of mob violence and adhere to the letter of the law. Their insistence on law and order prevented mob justice, but it couldn't prevent a crowd.

Despite Mitchell changing his story again at the last minute and recanting his confession, his execution took place on July 30. He was led to a scaffold

Thousands of spectators gathered outside the McLennan County Jail to witness the hanging of Roy Mitchell. *Lee Lockwood Library and Museum.*

that was erected behind the McLennan County Jail for what would be called the last public hanging carried out in the state of Texas. A crowd estimated to number between four and eight thousand people gathered outside the jail to hear Mitchell's last words: "Goodbye, everybody." Unlike the cases of Jesse Thomas and Jesse Washington, Mitchell's body was safeguarded by local authorities for burial. The crowd dispersed without recorded incident, and the end of a Waco serial killing spree was carried out in a legal manner, a tribute as much to local authorities as to the overwhelming public response to a nationwide NAACP anti-lynching campaign, which historian Bernstein points out was launched largely due to the "Waco Horror" of 1916.

Local historian Patricia Ward Wallace noted that while Mitchell's trial and execution were carried out in a legal manner, it would have been very unlikely that Mitchell could have received an entirely fair process from arrest to execution. She points out that due to the strong influence of the KKK in Waco during the early 1920s, as well as past mob justice actions against innocent men like Jesse Thomas, the public sentiment toward a black man accused of murdering five white people would be strongly negative, and pressure on the local authorities to "do something to right the wrong" would have been incredibly high.

Historians continue to debate whether Mitchell's public hanging was actually the last public execution in Texas. Some make a claim that the much less publicized hanging in August 1923 of a man named Nathan Lee in Angleton qualifies as the last example of a "public execution," but because of the lack of a crowd, it doesn't meet the textbook definition of "public." Regardless of its status as penultimate or ultimate, the execution of Roy Mitchell was a defining and now largely unknown event in 1920s-era Waco that would shape race relations in the city for decades to come.

A final note on this story is related in a 1997 article by Lori Lenarduzzi in the Baylor University *Lariat* student newspaper. She interviewed Kent Keeth, then director of The Texas Collection at Baylor, who said that former Waco mayor Roger Conger "had a piece of the rope that was used to hang Mitchell. I saw it many times." It was a macabre memento from a difficult moment in Waco history, no doubt, but also exactly the kind of thing that local historians would be expected to preserve for future generations.

4

The "Invisible Empire" on Austin Avenue

A Brief History of the KKK in Waco

The Ku Klux Klan experienced its second rebirth in the late 1910s and early 1920s, peaking with an estimated membership of two to four million in 1924. The first Klan emerged from the wounded pride of former Confederate soldiers and sought to terrorize freedmen and their allies and to influence the politics of Reconstruction across the South. After a hiatus of forty-plus years from 1871 to 1915, the Klan reemerged in its most recognizable form as a cadre of robed, cross-burning racists using hatred and violence to murder, plunder and generally terrorize a host of people whom they deemed undesirable: African Americans, Catholics, Jews and even divorced people. And at the height of the "Invisible Empire's" power, the Klan staged a Fourth of July parade down Austin Avenue, resulting in one of the most powerful and unsettling images of Waco's past.

Like other southern cities in the mid-1910s, Waco would develop a close relationship with the Klan. Owing both to its central location in the state and its history of embracing racist politics in the past, Waco was fertile ground for a local chapter, Saxet Klan Number 33, which sprang up around 1921 with Erwin J. Clark as the "Grand Titan of the Waco Province." Under his leadership, the Klan set about a formal process of recruiting members. Clark's efforts proved to be so successful they led to an overflow crowd for a 1921 initiation ceremony that brought more than nine hundred members into the group, with more than two hundred turned away for lack of space.

Efforts also included attempting to convince Protestant preachers to serve as "kludds" (the Klan version of a chaplain) by giving them free membership in the local chapter. They also exerted a strong hold over local commerce, according to the entry for the Ku Klux Klan in Waco from the Waco History site. They did this "by declaring that Klansmen were required to shop at Klan-owned stores and also to harass businesses owned by Catholics and Jews. To make these distinctions clear, a white card with black bars was displayed in the windows of Klan-friendly businesses around town."

Waco's reputation as a Klan-friendly town was further cemented in October 1921, when the local chapter, fresh off a successful parade in the nearby town of Mart, looked to stage a similar event in the town of Lorena, a few miles south of the city proper. In what would become known as the "Lorena Riot," more than four thousand people showed up to watch the event. What was unexpected was the insistence of McLennan County sheriff Bob Buchanan that the leaders of the group unmask themselves or he would deny them the opportunity to march. Klansmen, of course, never remove their hoods in public, so a tense standoff ensued, with Lorena locals attempting to convince Sheriff Buchanan to drop his demand.

The parade began over the sheriff's objections with a burning cross and an American flag leading the group as it marched forward with Klansmen arranged in rows, two by two. At some point, the sheriff attempted to remove a Klansman's hood; a shot rang out and weapons were drawn, and in the ensuing melee, a man named Louis Crow wound up dead, stabbed by a knife allegedly wielded by Sheriff Buchanan. Buchanan was indicted for Crow's murder, and in the 1922 election, the pro-Klan sentiment in McLennan County was high enough to result in a Ku Klux Klan ticket winning countywide offices, including that of sheriff.

One additional major Klan-related action took place in Waco at this time. The KKK in Waco entry on Waco History puts it this way:

> *The KKK then set its sights on higher political office: the state senate. In what was known as the "Waco Agreement," four Grand Titans met in Waco at the Raleigh Hotel to decide which senate candidate the Klan would support. Three different Klansmen were in the running at the time, so it was not a straightforward decision. They decided to let the Klan choose by declaring an open race with the understanding that the trailing Klansmen would drop out when the time came. One of the candidates, Wacoan Robert Henry, ran openly as a Klansman, showing the legitimacy of the KKK at the state and national level. Klan officials ended up reneging the Waco Agreement and supporting Earle Mayfield, who did not run openly as a Klansman, over Henry and the third candidate Sterling Strong because of*

his ties to big business. Mayfield went on to win the Democratic primary. But the agreement and Henry's candidacy show the extent to which Waco was a center for Klan authority.

After its statewide effort to control the capitol came to naught, the Klan experienced a drop-off in popularity almost as precipitous as its original rise was meteoric. An openly pro-Klan candidate lost a run-off for governor against Miriam "Ma" Ferguson, and people's concerns over the "low-class" influence of some newer Klan members caused respectable people to distance themselves from the group and its increasingly mob-fueled activities. As the Waco History entry notes, by 1927, the Klan had sold all of its Waco property, and aside from an occasional blip on the radar screen of history—such as when a Wacoan named Horace Sherman Miller started a "mail-order" chapter of the Aryan Knights of the KKK from his home in the early 1950s—the KKK and Waco parted ways for good by the start of the Great Depression.

This photo captures one of the last large Klan parades held in Waco, a Fourth of July display of masked audacity marching down Austin Avenue, the heart of the city's thriving downtown. It is a stark, harshly lit image of

The KKK staged several large parades in the Waco area in the early 1920s, like this one down Austin Avenue on July 4, 1924. *Lee Lockwood Library and Museum.*

hate personified, surrounded by thousands of curious onlookers and—if the numbers of documented KKK sympathizers nationwide at this time are to be believed—not a few people who saw the display as perfectly fitting for part of the city's Independence Day celebration. According to a master's thesis by Baylor University student Richard Fair, the Klan participated in this way as a show of strength after a Klan-supported candidate, Felix Robertson, won a victory in the Democratic primary election for governor. Their electoral success put them in a mood to celebrate what they saw as "anticipation of future victory."

The Klansmen are stopped in ranks near the front of the Hippodrome Theatre at 724 Austin. Behind the first grouping of approximately two dozen Klansmen are two figures mounted on horseback, followed by a line of robed men stretching into the far distance. Most of the men at the head of the parade are wearing only hoods and masks covering the upper portion of their faces; those from the horsemen on back are wearing full hoods and face masks.

While most of the onlookers are focused on the spectacle before them, a few have turned back in the direction of the unnamed photographer, whose rig must have been set up directly in the center of the intersection of Austin Avenue and Eighth Street. It is obvious from the lack of motion on the Klan's part that this photo opportunity was anticipated, and the forward momentum of the group was brought to a halt here, at the nexus of downtown, to best memorialize the Klan's massed malevolence. The image is one of eerie stillness, a large group of curiosity-seekers surrounding anonymous men whose appearance on an important American holiday was intentional, calculated and effective.

IV

Stories of Postwar Waco

I

A Herculean Work

The Secret Birth and Largely Forgotten Legacy of Sironia, Texas

When most people think of long literary works, their minds likely go to the Bible (roughly 1,200 pages), *Gone with the Wind* (1,037 pages) or *War and Peace* (1,225 pages). Far fewer, even among the Waco citizenry, would call to mind the name *Sironia, Texas*. However, weighing in at a hefty 1,731 pages and a shade over one million words, Madison Cooper Jr.'s novel about the waxing and waning fortunes of several families in a fictional town with a strong resemblance to Waco is one of the longest books ever published in the English language. And for a brief eleven-week period in 1952—the year it was released by Houghton Mifflin—it found itself on the *New York Times* bestseller list, despite being an extremely dense, complicated and even divisive work of thinly veiled satire.

To understand *Sironia, Texas* it is important to know more about its reclusive author. Madison Cooper Jr. was born in Waco in 1894 to a family that had made its mark on the local business scene thanks to the success of the M.A. Cooper Company, a large wholesale grocery concern. By all accounts, Cooper was a good student; he attended the University of Texas at Austin and earned a degree in English in 1915. After a brief stint working at his family's company, Cooper enlisted in the U.S. Army and served in World War I. After the war, he returned home to Waco to continue working in the family business.

Cooper was known as an eccentric man. A lifelong bachelor, he showed no interest in the obvious trappings of wealth and privilege his status as the scion of one of Waco's richest families could offer him. He lived with his parents in a stunning home at Eighteenth and Austin Avenues that was built in 1907 to his father's exacting standards for sturdiness and aesthetic appeal. He wore clothes far beyond their useful lifespan, with a shabby cardigan sweater cited as one of his trademark pieces. He carried a weather-beaten briefcase and walked all over town in ragged shoes. He was polite and unfailingly modest, with a heart for helping people in his hometown that would show itself on a grand scale in years to come.

What few people knew at the time was that Cooper harbored ambitions beyond the local business world. Few—if any—knew that he had begun writing short stories under a pseudonym, Matt Cooper, and he had enrolled in correspondence courses on writing offered by Columbia University. But his small successes in selling his stories would remain just that—small—until a series of family deaths occurred in the late 1930s and early 1940s. His mother, Martha, passed away in 1939, and his father, Madison Sr., died in 1940.

Whether the deaths of his parents broke loose a psychic logjam or if in response to the grief he felt at their dying he was spurred to action on an ambition long held is unclear, but the fact remains that in 1941 he began writing what would come to be his legacy to the literary world. According to his biographer Marion Travis, Cooper got the idea of writing a magnum opus about a fictionalized southern town after he wrote a short story called "The Catch of Sironia." He spent the next eleven years—from 1941 to 1952—working on *Sironia, Texas* in a small attic space he renovated in his father's house for the express purpose of providing a refuge for writing. The room remains to this day in the same state it was in when Cooper died in 1956, with his papers, a Waco telephone directory and other ephemera remaining in situ for more than sixty years.

Sironia, Texas was published by a powerful literary firm, Houghton Mifflin, in 1952, much to the surprise of people in Waco who viewed Cooper as a reclusive, middle-aged man of means living in a stunning Victorian mansion on one of the city's main drags. It was welcomed with largely mixed reviews: some praised its ability to satirize life in a southern town bridging the Reconstruction era and the rise of the middle class in the early twentieth century. Others claimed it was notable only for its length and showed a roughness of skill. Regardless, the book spent eleven weeks on the *New York Times* bestseller list before disappearing from the charts.

What caused its precipitous fall? Opinions differ, but most agree that it came down to cost—ten dollars for a two-volume work in 1952 meant spending the equivalent of ninety-six dollars for a book in 2019—and its

Madison Cooper Jr. poses with the typescript manuscript of *Sironia, Texas*, circa 1952. *Lee Lockwood Museum and Library.*

incredible length and complexity did not help. Another factor working against *Sironia, Texas* was the competition it faced from other authors, notably Ernest Hemingway's *The Old Man and the Sea* and *East of Eden* by John Steinbeck. Despite its widespread release from a major publisher, copies of *Sironia, Texas* are hard to come by today, especially the two-volume version first printed in 1952; collectors regularly spend hundreds of dollars to acquire a copy.

So what is *Sironia, Texas* about? The simple answer is: a lot. After spending many months working my way through its complex narrative, and without spoiling the work for anyone intrigued enough to seek it out, it's easiest to say that *Sironia, Texas* is a work of fiction drawn from the observations and internal calculus of a thoughtful man who saw a city he loved go through tremendous social and economic change over the course of half a century. It is the story of a dying way of life, the antebellum South, as represented by the "Hill families," the original settlers of Sironia, whose wealth stretches back to the late 1800s but is on the decline as the novel progresses. It is also the story of the up-and-coming business class, represented by the family of a shopkeeper whose status in town may be shaped by his wealth but is kept in check because he doesn't come from the "old stock."

Sironia, Texas is also a novel about race, and it treats this subject with more compassion and nuance than one might expect for a novel written some fifteen years before the civil rights movement. African American characters make up a good percentage of the novel's massive list of characters, as do other biracial characters (often servants of the Hill families or children born of illicit affairs between rich white and poor black Sironians). The dialect of many black characters is rendered throughout in a way similar to the approach taken by Mark Twain, with words spelled more to reflect the way they sounded to a listener and not in a manner suited to making for easier reading. Black characters are given significant roles in the advancement of the story and internal motivations that reflect a conflict between seeking new opportunities—such as one character's struggle with whether to leave town to attend college—and staying in Sironia to be one of the "good Negroes" who works for a "good white" family. At times, the dialogue is difficult for modern readers to digest, with its frequent use of the "n-word" and some cringingly painful attempts to document a former slave's laugh ("hyah-hyah-hyah" is one version), but overall, Cooper treats his black characters with a level of respect and attention that is refreshingly admirable.

There is plenty of fantasy woven throughout the novel as well, from an appearance by a horseback-riding ghost to a fire in a brothel and a great deal of (mostly undescribed) teenage visions of what sex is like. There are also numerous masterful passages describing the material culture and social mores of a society long gone by, from descriptions of opulent parlors and their furnishings to long passages about social gatherings like dances and community meetings. There is even a group modeled on the Ku Klux Klan (the Southern Patriots) and a subplot involving a prostitute who returns to town after leaving Sironia under a cloud of suspicion.

With all of this activity packed into its 1,700-plus pages, it's also disappointing to report that, for this reader at least, *Sironia, Texas* is a very, very slow read. There are dozens of major characters whose interactions form the basis of the main plot, and it is paced over the course of decades. There are many interminable passages where Cooper renders extreme detail about a setting, or a piece of clothing, or a stand of trees, but the plot will advance not a foot for the span of twenty or more pages before suddenly lurching forward at breakneck speed in the final paragraphs of a chapter. It is, at best, an uneven work and, at worst, an exasperating one.

In my unprofessional literary opinion, there are aspects of Waco that are obvious in the novel, particularly in the two characters of Tam Lipscomb and Launcelot "Mr. Lance" Thaxton. Lipscomb is the son of a dry goods store owner, a member of the nouveau riche and the expected heir to the family fortune. Thaxton is a son of one of the major Hill families, once all-powerful but in decline by the second half of the book. He is written as someone with a combination of personality traits that indicate either mental handicap or perhaps an autism spectrum disorder: he is described as childlike, gentle and oblivious to the machinations of his mother, who attempts to marry him off to a number of eligible bachelorettes, to no avail. Notably, he is described as wandering the streets in increasingly tattered clothing, walking for hours and spending his time either mowing his family's expansive grounds or puttering away in a workshop. Both Lipscomb and Thaxton seem to represent significant portions of Cooper's own personality, a way of inserting the author into the work in ways that would have been obvious to those who knew him.

Despite its challenging aspects, *Sironia, Texas* had an almost immediate effect on the people of Waco, including the many residents who chose not to shell out almost one hundred dollars and spend hundreds of hours reading it. Within weeks of its release, major newspapers were suggesting that the book's major characters were based on people Cooper knew from his hometown. Rumors began to circulate about prominent families and their peccadillos being exposed in a "satirical" novel that was so thinly veiled as to be impossible to deny. But deny it Cooper did, claiming repeatedly that the characters in *Sironia, Texas* were constructions of his imagining and that the novel bore only the loosest resemblance to Waco society.

Cooper wrote a follow-up novel called *The Haunted Hacienda* that was a much more reasonable three hundred pages, but it did not register with the public, and plans for future works were put on hold. Cooper continued his reclusive existence and stuck to a schedule that included regularly jogging

The desk where Cooper wrote *Sironia, Texas* has been kept exactly as he left it on the day of his death in 1956. *Author's collection.*

A collection of shops on Austin Avenue, just blocks from the Cooper mansion, operates under the Sironia name. *Author's collection.*

at the Waco Municipal Stadium. He had just finished his workout on September 28, 1956, when he returned to his car, sat down in the passenger seat, had a massive heart attack and died at age sixty-two.

The legacy of Cooper's "not so secret" novel about Waco and its people is evident in a few key ways today. One is the persistent rumor that Cooper had a "key" to the characters in the novel and their real-life counterparts, possibly hidden on the back of a map in his attic workroom. (Incidentally, on a research trip I took to the home, my guide, Kelly Ezell, pointed out a number of maps hanging in the room, which happened to be of Cooper family landholdings outside of Waco. Perhaps these were the inspiration for the aforementioned "character key map?") Another, more visible, remainder is the collection of vendors and artists operating out of a space called Sironia, located just down Austin Avenue from Cooper's former home.

But Cooper's legacy for the city of Waco goes far beyond his literary one. In 1943, he established the Cooper Foundation in memory of his parents. Dedicated to making Waco "a better place in which to live," the foundation began by giving small donations to community groups while Cooper was alive. Upon his death, the entirety of his estate went to the foundation, and the family home was designated its headquarters. As of 2015, the Cooper Foundation has distributed more than $24 million to better the lives of Wacoans—whether they were the models for a resident of Sironia or not.

2

The William Cameron House

Born of Love, Haunted by Loss

While we are on the subject of wealthy Waco families and their extravagant houses, it's worth recounting an interesting story related to the palatial manse of one William Cameron, a Scottish immigrant who made his fortune in the timber and lumber industries. In the early 1880s, he struck upon the idea of building an immense new home for his second wife, Flora. He commissioned French architect W.W. Larmour—whose notable local works included Old Main and Burleson Halls at Baylor University, Sacred Heart Academy and the R.T. Dennis Furniture Company—to construct an emphatic Victorian-style edifice at 1223 Austin Avenue as a surprise to Flora.

When it was completed in 1885, the resulting home was a triumph of Victorian asymmetry, with a stately central tower, elaborate wooden ornamentation and enough square footage to house a battalion of infantry. The Cameron family and their hired staff made the mansion their home beyond William's death in 1899, when it was inherited by his son William Waldo Cameron. When W.W. Cameron died, it came into the possession of Edward Cameron Bolton, a grandson of William Cameron. Bolton saw only the trouble of keeping up the maintenance on a house of such immense size, so he sold it to the Coca-Cola Bottling Company, which planned to raze the structure and construct a new facility on the prime piece of Austin Avenue real estate it occupied.

In 1966, before the edifice was scheduled to be demolished, it was decided that the house's architectural elements—everything from windowsills to mantelpieces, the iron cupola to mahogany floorboards—would be sold by a young man named Homer Owen. Owen saw an additional opportunity to make some extra money by charging curious Wacoans an admission fee to tour the house. Eventually, the lure of easy access proved a problem when vandals broke into the house and caused damage to some of the remaining furnishings. According to a June 25, 1966 article in the *Waco Tribune-Herald* by Tommy West, Owen decided to spend a night in the house to keep it secure. Owen, West wrote, "lay awake until dawn with a shotgun in his hand listening to 'strange noises.'" And so the ghost stories began.

A series of other hardy souls attempted to spend the night in the Cameron House, each of whom found it difficult to impossible to sleep: college students, a carpenter, even Owen's own business partner. All of them either quit before the night was through or, in the carpenter's case, "went out and stayed drunk for three days." The most common complaint was of a series of "strange noises," although Owen and his partner both claim they heard voices coming from the top floor. Further evidence of supernatural shenanigans included a closet door that refused to stay shut; inside were old wedding clothes that had likely belonged to the original owners of the home. Each time Owen tried to shut them into the closet, he found it open again the next morning.

According to West's article, speculation was soon rampant that the ghost was none other than W.W. Larmour, the architect who designed the house. The thinking went that because several of Larmour's most prominent buildings had been either destroyed—like Sacred Heart and the R.T. Dennis Company—or severely altered, as in the case of the Old Main bell towers, Larmour was having his revenge on the city of Waco by haunting one of the remaining vestiges of his once dominant architectural genius. Others believed the ghostly goings-on were related to the spirits of William Cameron's beloved dogs, one of whom was said to have begun acting strangely at the precise time Cameron died while on a trip to Louisiana. Whatever their source, the paranormal activity at the Cameron House was strong enough to deter even the most determined of overnight visitors.

There is another explanation for the sudden spike in ghost stories surrounding the home. As proffered by former *Waco Tribune-Herald* writer Marion Travis, the first reports of ghostly noises surfaced only after interest in the home had waned following a few strong weeks of tours and sales of its architectural elements. Perhaps, she suggested in a Fall 1979 edition of *Waco Heritage & History*, there never was a ghost at all, but the demolition team "found an opportunity for some fun, or if the ghost story evolved to stimulate traffic through the house. Perhaps all three were factors."

In the midst of all this supernatural speculation, one fact regarding the final days of the Cameron House is undeniable. In the early morning hours of June 30, 1966, something combustible burst into flames inside the massive edifice, causing a fire that burned the majority of the structure to the ground. Opinions are divided over whether it was caused by faulty electrical wiring, vandals or an otherworldly cause; what is undeniable is that shortly after the fire, the remains were bulldozed away, and the Coca-Cola Company had its plot of land ready for new construction.

In her *Waco Heritage & History* article, Travis wrote, "Today the William Cameron House, completely unsuited to the times in the place where it once stood, has been consigned to memory and the history books, where it still can please those exploring the past." For those of us documenting Waco's history in the present who were not around to witness its elegance and impressive size for ourselves, her description and those of her contemporaries are the only reminders we have—unless there are any remaining ghosts lingering around the now-vacant Coca-Cola facility that stands at 1223 Austin Avenue.

3

Towering Above the Brazos Once Again

Restoring Baylor's Old Main Towers

Careful readers of the previous entry on the William Cameron House will recognize the reappearance here of a key figure from that tragic building's past: William Winant Larmour, the French-born architect who dreamed up and executed its blue-and-white Victorian excesses. Larmour made quite a name for himself in Waco as the mind behind a number of imposing edifices, but today only a scant few remain. Fortunately for today's fans of nineteenth-century architecture, one of the survivors is a pair of buildings on the Baylor University campus: Old Main and Burleson Hall. These redbrick buildings anchor the center of Baylor's historic core and today are home to offices and classrooms, but for a brief time following a devastating natural disaster they were without their most recognizable feature: their towers.

Former Baylor faculty member Daniel Reiff, in a 1967 article, described the buildings as "not simply contractor-built piles of brick, but rather [they] reflect an important movement in American architecture with a distinctive style all [their] own," and he noted their towers lent a "Gothic character" to their silhouettes. Larmour's design certainly elevated Old Main and Burleson into a class of architecture sometimes referred to as "academic Victorian" or "collegiate Gothic," an attempt at marrying the quotidian needs of instructors—like large, functional classrooms—with the aspirational hopes of administrators. In short, Larmour set out to design buildings that would help Baylor educate the minds of its students while uplifting their spirits through architectural excellence.

But beauty alone cannot justify unnecessary risk, and that's exactly how the towers came to be viewed in the wake of one of Waco's most newsworthy events: a devastating F5 tornado that struck downtown on May 11, 1953, killing 114 people and causing millions of dollars in damage to properties large and small. Baylor's campus was spared the tornado's wrath, but the fear of what could have happened if fate drove the storm just a mile east of its final path give university president W.R. White enough concern that he ordered the towers removed. He wrote in an article in the *Waco Tribune-Herald* the year of the tornado, "If the May tornado had cut across the Baylor campus, there is a possibility the towers would have crumbled to the ground….There is a continuing danger that in case of other high winds the tall spires might collapse, falling either through the building roof or across the campus walks. We dare not take that chance."

The original towers were removed from Old Main and Burleson Hall shortly after White's decision was made public, and for twenty-two years the buildings sported flat-topped stubs where once mighty spires had towered above the campus. In the 1960s through the early 1970s, intense debates were held among administrators, students, planners and architectural preservationists about the future of Baylor's oldest buildings. There were strong calls to demolish them and replace them with a new, modern library (a structure that would come to open in 1968 on land acquired by the university as part of Waco's urban renewal project, thus sparing Old Main and Burleson from the wrecking ball). In 1973, the board of trustees received a presentation from an architectural firm on the future of the buildings that included erecting a new structure between the two (today's Draper Hall) that would house classrooms and offices and thus preserve Old Main and Burleson for future generations. A part of that plan also called for the restoration of the buildings' towers.

From the outset, Baylor's engineers worked to restore the towers' original look and feel but with upgrades to the infrastructure that would help secure them against even a catastrophic twister's winds. The towers themselves were constructed of wood covered with turn-metal shingles, along with a steel base that connects to a steel substructure that was extended down into the original brick walls of the building, providing additional stability for both the towers and the exterior walls they sit upon.

On the project's completion in 1975, architect Harold Calhoun—a member of the firm who did the restoration work—said, "When the last tower was finally placed on the buildings in October, I felt the deep satisfaction of having helped to restore for the pleasure of students, faculty, alumni and the general public one of the landmarks of Waco history—and made it useful for the present generation as well." And while future renovations to Old Main and Burleson would go on to alter the building's character by adding modern windows in place of its original four-over-four, double-hung sash windows, the effort to restore their most defining characteristics was a complete—and historically accurate—success.

4
The Stories We Tell

The (So Far) Missed Opportunity of the Taylor Museum

One of the most-asked questions from visitors when planning a trip to Waco is "Where is the local history museum?" The answer to that question depends on who you ask. The Mayborn Museum features information about the Central Texas area, but its Waco-centric offerings are scant. The Dr Pepper Museum, the Waco Police Museum, The Texas Collection at Baylor University and Historic Waco Foundation all tell parts of the Waco story. But no single institution tells the expansive history of Waco, from the Native American era to the present, in a comprehensive display of Waco history. That was the gap that the Helen Marie Taylor Museum: The Life and History of Waco (or, more succinctly, the Taylor Museum) attempted to fill when it opened in 1993. But as with many institutions envisioned and created by a dominant personality, the promise of a one-stop shop for Waco history proved to be elusive, and the city's best hope for a cohesive narrative of Waco's history has languished in a purgatory of its own making for more than twenty years.

For good or ill, the story of the Taylor Museum can be attributed almost single-handedly to Helen Marie Taylor, a Waco native with ancestral ties to two former U.S. presidents (Zachary Taylor and James Madison). Long interested in history both local and national, Taylor was involved with various civic groups when she began stumping for a new local history museum following the dedication of the Historic Waco Foundation's McCulloch House in 1980. According to an article in the *Houston Chronicle* in 2002, Taylor remembers that she "made a very eloquent plea to the people gathered there…to go a few blocks and look at this old abandoned school. I suggested because of its historic significance, it would make a wonderful civic museum. The problem was the only person who was truly, deeply moved by what I had to say was me."

Taylor was speaking of the former Barron Springs Elementary School, situated at a deeply significant geographic area of Waco encompassing a former Native American camping spot, several major oaks dated to be more than five hundred years old and the school itself, a former African American school that operated as such until Waco underwent integration following the civil rights era. It is also only blocks away from a historically Latino neighborhood, giving the site of the Taylor Museum the unique opportunity to tell the stories of Native Americans, African Americans, Latinos and Anglo settlers, all in one convenient location. When Taylor bought the building in 1986—for "practically a dollar" as she put it during a recent speech given at an award ceremony honoring her commitment to the site—she wasted little time in holding a groundbreaking (1989) and grand opening (1993).

The museum's extensive name is based, she claims, on an error in paperwork. As she formed the vision for her Waco museum, she was initially inspired by museums dedicated to her predecessors, particularly James Madison, whose legacy is celebrated in Orange, Virginia, at the James Madison Museum of Orange County Heritage. Taylor claims that in the incorporating paperwork, "someone" wrote the official name as the Helen Marie Taylor Museum: The Life and History of Waco, and before she caught the mistake, it was too late to change it. While this version of events is impossible to verify, it is widely argued that putting her own name on the institution set in motion the public sentiment that the museum was "created by Helen Marie Taylor for Halen Marie Taylor," as former Baylor University Museum Studies faculty member Calvin Smith told the *Chronicle* article's author, Michelle Hillen.

What is undeniable is the fact that when it opened in 1993, the Taylor Museum's purported focus on the "life and history" of Waco proved to be only partial, with a significant amount of the museum's square footage dedicated to the American colonial era and the American republic. Artifacts in the "We the People" section of the museum—clearly intended to be the museum's most important showcase—included a heavy focus on the Constitution and colonial-era "great white men." In addition to a re-creation of the room where the Constitutional Convention was held (including a chair from the actual event), the exhibit contained a Revolutionary War musket and a silk vest that belonged to George Washington. Although the exhibit received positive reviews from early visitors, word quickly spread that the museum spent a significant amount of the visitor's time engaged in events that took place a full century or more before Waco's founding in 1849, despite Taylor's insistence that there could be no Waco history without American colonial history, a statement that is factually true as it relates to Anglo settlement but omits the entire span of Native Americans' involvement with the Waco area, which dates back centuries.

While the inclusion of pieces focusing on Taylor's personal interests could have been accepted as a bit of founder's privilege, the omission of significant aspects of Waco's past could not. Major events like the 1953 tornado, the history of the suspension bridge (one of Waco's greatest triumphs and an important civic icon), the full history of Waco's academic life (including once being home to Paul Quinn College, a historically black college), not to mention the lack of minority voices from Latinos, African Americans and Jewish Wacoans, doomed the museum to a reputation of telling only part of the story: specifically, the story that Helen Marie Taylor wanted to tell.

Tensions between Taylor and her board of directors, exacerbated by a deteriorating financial situation, caused the museum to close to the public in 1998. At the time, Taylor claimed she was invested for $5 million, including a "$2.5 million loan that she had expected Waco volunteers to repay through fundraising efforts," according to the 2002 *Chronicle* article. In the ensuing two decades, there have been multiple attempts to reopen the Taylor Museum. Just a year after it closed, former backers attempted to arrange a deal wherein the museum would reopen, but the sticking points remained Taylor's insistence on keeping part of the focus on colonial American artifacts—and the repayment of the $2.5 million loan. In 2009, the *Waco Tribune-Herald*'s J.B. Smith reported that Taylor was in talks with the Historic Waco Foundation, but they came to nothing after Taylor once again refused to budge on her vision for the museum. Regarding an updated vision for the museum's focus, Taylor said during negotiations with HWF, "We will not be unreasonable about it. But I don't want some fool telling me the whole second floor should be torn out....Kids don't stop being born, and people don't stop needing to know about the Constitution," she added.

A series of public events held in 2018 and 2019, along with the announcement of the "hiring" of a new director—who was unpaid and had no previous museum experience—in 2017, gave brief glimmers of hope that the museum could one day reopen, but as of this writing, the museum remains mostly closed. (The new director lasted only a few months on the job before parting ways with the museum.) Visitors who manage to

The Texas centennial marker on the grounds of the Taylor Museum. The secondary marker from 2014 corrects information on the 1936 original. *Author's collection.*

reach the caretaker by phone in advance of their arrival to the site may score one of the coveted private tours, but most settle on wandering the museum's grounds and marveling at the centuries-old oak trees and the 1936 Texas Centennial marker that celebrates the Waco Indians and their history with the site.

But even something as brief as the write-up on the marker isn't without its own controversy. In 2014, a group of researchers added a second plaque to the original marker. The new plaque corrects historical inaccuracies about the Wacos and their interactions with other tribes, as well as the false story that the Wacos made a treaty with Stephen F. Austin. Now, visitors to the site can read the original text on the 1936 marker and the corrected information just below it. And perhaps that approach—respecting original intent and providing new insight based on current scholarship—is the perfect model for how to reinvigorate the Helen Marie Taylor Museum: The Life and History of Waco. But interested parties will have to act quickly: the opportunity to work with its fiercely independent ninety-five-year-old founder is slipping away as quickly as the memories of the Revolutionary era she holds so dear.

V

Lagniappe, or, Sometimes a Hidden Story Remains Unexplained

Despite my best efforts throughout this work, there are some photos I encountered in various archives for which no suitable explanation could be found. They remain frustratingly unanswered, with just enough information to make them approachable but, at least for now, unknowable. Sometimes you can identify a participant, or a location, but not a date or a reason; sometimes, all you get is a short note scribbled on the reverse that points to some piece of Waco history that was important enough to document with a camera but not important enough to document in words. In this section, I'll provide what I know about a few of these tantalizing glimpses into the recesses of Waco's past, but know this, dear reader: what is seen cannot be unseen, and what is experienced here will not be fully explained (at least not in this volume).

The notation on this photograph identifies the man sporting a Stetson and two six-shooters as William Smith Hammond, the father-in-law of "Mr. Waco History" (and former Waco mayor) Roger Conger. The two men in Native American dress are not identified, though circumstantial evidence points to their being presented as authentic Waco Indians (or close enough as to fool the intended audience for this photo). The only other piece of identifiable information presented is that the building in the background is Waco City Hall.

The image bears all the hallmarks of a publicity photo, though whatever event it was intended to promote is not noted. Despite the presence of numerous firearms and a large knife, the outward appearances of the three men are friendly, if not a bit bemused by their being instructed to point

Above: William S. Hammond (*left*) poses with two unidentified men in Native American–style clothing outside Waco City Hall, undated. *Lee Lockwood Library and Museum.*

Opposite, top: A large commercial kitchen captured after hours by Fred Gildersleeve, undated. *Lee Lockwood Library and Museum.*

Opposite, bottom: A "William Cameron Co. meeting," undated. *Lee Lockwood Library and Museum.*

weapons at one another in what could be best described as a staged moment of protocosplay.

This photo of a large, well-stocked restaurant kitchen was likely part of Gildersleeve's ongoing efforts to document working-class Waco, particularly the commercial concerns that reflected Waco's thriving economy in the early twentieth century. The restaurant is unidentified, and the slogan on the far back left wall—"The Largest, Best Lighted, Most Sanitary, Best Equipped Kitchen"—is partially obscured enough as to make it unhelpful for identification purposes. Wherever it was located, management had an interest in maintaining an orderly kitchen staff, judging by the proclamation on the center column: "Profane or boisterous language positively prohibited in this kitchen."

Gildersleeve
Waco

Courtesy
Quality
Service
LEARN TO RIDE YOUR CUSTOMERS' HOBBIES
Smiles
Industry
Results
THIS IS FOR THE DEAD ONES
SATISFACTION
Gildersleeve
Waco

It's hard to know where to start with this particular photo, which is described only as "William Cameron Lumber Co. meeting" in the catalogue records of the Lockwood Library and Museum, where it is part of the Gildersleeve collection. If this is indeed a meeting, it's hard to imagine it's a regular Monday morning staff get-together, unless those routinely involved men dressed as babies, skeletons and gremlins or another man seated on a toilet mounted to a rolling platform.

The men captured in this photo—and it is almost entirely an all-male affair, with the exception of one woman, seen standing next to a man in a stroller dressed as a baby—are ranged around a large room with wooden floors and a tin roof; a backdrop of sorts is visible in the background bearing the crest of the Cameron Highlanders. The crowd is grouped into several distinct sections around the perimeter of the room. There is a group dressed in academic robes; a pair of gremlins; a group of Highlanders in kilts, along with a pair of men in medieval armor; several men in what appear to be their underwear; two men in business suits; and two wearing white robes and large skull masks. There are signs around the room bearing what are either business-related slogans ("Learn to ride your customers' hobbies" and "courtesy" are two examples) or cryptic messages. (The skull men hold a sign that reads "This is for the dead ones," while the man dressed as a baby holds a sign reading "Better Babies Make Better Men.")

The thematic groupings of the men in the room, along with the theatrical trappings on display and the (one assumes) intentionally over-the-top symbolism of the whole affair give it the appearance of a group dressed for a parade or public performance, or as part of an internal team-building exercise but with a higher than usual concentration of absurdity. While the meaning of the image is unclear to modern viewers, the overall message is one of a large group of men, focused on a singular vision, who are willing to go to great lengths to accomplish whatever their common objective may have been at the time the photo was captured. It is a true pity we will likely never know what that purpose was.

Bibliography

This book would not exist were it not for the efforts of previous authors, journalists, historians and documenters of Waco's past whose works I relied upon to craft this collection of disparate stories into a cohesive whole. Below are my citations for each section; I encourage all who are interested in Waco's past to seek them out, read them and find in them the same enjoyment I did.

Part I

Reflections of "Days Agone" by a Waco Lawyer circa 1876

Herring, Marcus D. "Historical Sketch of Waco." *Waco Heritage & History*, Winter 1974.

Waco Register. July 8, 1876.

"Waco Three Decades Agone." *Waco Heritage & History*, Summer 1971.

Waco Celebrates the American Centennial

Waco Daily Examiner. July 2, 1876.

Waco Heritage & History, Summer 1974.

Waco Register. "The Centennial Fourth of July Celebration at Waco." July 8, 1876.

"Geyser City": Artesian Wells and the Water Cure

Culler's Guide to the City of Waco. 1894.

Miller, Sarah. "Waco Natatorium." wacohistory.org.

Smith, J.B. "La Pila Fountain Once Central to Hispanic Neighborhood Unearthed." *Waco Tribune-Herald*, June 22, 2017.

Waco Morning News. April 9, 1889.

———. "Half of City Water from Artesian Wells." March 23, 1915.

———. "Waco, the Geyser City." March 18, 1892.

Waco News-Tribune. Advertising section. October 6, 1928.

———. "Owners of Land Needed for Lake Make Low Price." August 25, 1926.

Waco Tribune-Herald. "First Waco Dam Brought Bitter Dispute, Splitting the Community." October 26, 1975.

The Tantalizing (and Disastrous) Dream of Steamboats on the Brazos

Waco Heritage & History. "The 'Kate Ross' and the 'Lizzie Fisher'—The Only Steamboats Seen Here. Their History and Fate. *Waco Weekly Tribune*, June 3, 1905." Reproduced in Summer 1971.

William Cowper Brann: Sinner's Saint, False Prophet or Journalistic Crusader?

Balwin, Helen. "The Personal Touch." *Waco Tribune-Herald*, May 9, 1954.

Brann, Mrs. W.C. (Carrie Belle Martin Brann). *Brann, The Iconoclast: A Collection of the Writings of W.C. Brann*. Waco, TX: Herz Brothers, 1911.

Lomax, John Nova. "The Apostle of the Devil." *Texas Monthly*, June 2016. texasmonthly.com.

Snow, Richard F. "American Characters: William Cowper Brann." *American Heritage* 30, no 4. (June/July 1979).

Waco Citizen. "Iconoclast Lives Again in Waco." August 24, 1990.

Waco History. "William Cowper Brann." wacohistory.org.

Waco Morning News. Advertisement for "Brann the Iconoclast" two-volume edition. October 24, 1911.

———. February 23, 1892.

———. June 15, 1895.

———. "William Cowper Brann, Painter, Printer[,] Reporter, Withal Foremost Editor." March 31, 1912.

Waco News-Tribune. "Tom Mix to Put Wreath on Grave of W.C. Brann." September 11, 1929.

Telephus Telemachus Louis Augustus Albartus "Tel" Johnson and His Famous Tombs

Tarleton State University. "About Us." www.tarleton.edu.

Texas State Historical Association. *Southwestern Historical Quarterly* 50 (June 1951–April 1952).

Travis, Marion. "Reclaiming Cemetery Tedious but Rewarding." *Waco News-Tribune*, September 19, 1968.

Waco News-Tribune. "Austin Street a Mudhole and Hogs Ran Wild Back in 1874." May 25, 1924.

Part II

The Fabulous Hoffmannettes and A Waco Romance

Waco News-Tribune. Advertisement for Hoffman Dance Studio. September 30, 1928.

———. "Memorial Dedication Honors Hoffmannettes." May 2, 1973.

———. "Shimmie! Nix, Say These." October 5, 1919.

Waco Tribune-Herald. "Pageant to Feature 1913 Movie." March 16, 1975.

Waco's Pride: Her Fire Department

"Souvenir booklet" of Waco Fire Department. Reproduced in winter 1970 issue of *Waco Heritage & History*.

Fred Gildersleeve's Eye for Waco

Conger, Roger. "Gildy Remembered." *Waco Heritage & History*, Winter 1976.

Hunt, Geoff, and Sarah Miller. "Fred Gildersleeve." wacohistory.org.

Waco Tribune-Herald. "Fred Gildersleeve Got His Picture, but Flash Almost Blew the Roof Off." October 15, 1961.

"The Church That Was Built in a Day"

Waco Citizen. "Church Built in Day Celebrates Anniversary." January 13, 1961.

Waco Morning News. "Methodist Congregations Are Richly Influential." October 31, 1915.

Part III

The "Little Rough Riders"

Find a Grave. "John Wescomb 'Jack' Parnum." findagrave.com.
Lindsey, Mary Edmond. "The Little Rough Riders." *Waco Heritage & History*, Winter 1979.

Waco's Refined Presence on a Merciless Dreadnought

Taylor, Lonn. "Sterling Success." *Texas Monthly*, May 2015.
Wikipedia. "USS *Texas* (BB-35)." wikipedia.org.

The Hanging of Roy Mitchell: Likely the Last Public Execution in Texas

Bernstein, Patricia. *The First Waco Horror: The Lynching of Jesse Washington and the Rise of the NAACP*. College Station: Texas A&M University Press, 2006.
Lenarduzzi, Lori. "Mitchell Murder Trial of 1923 Ended with Last Texas Hanging." *Baylor Lariat*, September 25, 1997.
Newton, Michael. *Hunting Humans: An Encyclopedia of Modern Serial Killers*. Port Townsend, WA: Loompanics Unlimited, 1990.

The "Invisible Empire" on Austin Avenue: A Brief History of the KKK in Waco

Burke, Anabel. "The Ku Klux Klan in Waco." wacohistory.org.
Fair, Richard H. "'The Good Angel of Practical Fraternity': The Ku Klux Klan in McLennan County, 1915–1924." Master's thesis, Baylor University, 2009.

Part IV

A Herculean Work: The Secret Birth and Largely Forgotten Legacy of Sironia, Texas

Barr, Michael. "The Great Wacoan Novel." *Texas Highways*, November 2015.
Holley, Joe. "Cooper Name Is Iconic; His Novel, Less So." *Houston Chronicle*, March 29, 2014.
Travis, Marion. *Madison Cooper*. Waco, TX: Word Inc., 1951.
———. "Waco Has a Hero." *Waco Heritage & History*, Fall 1980.

The William Cameron House: Born of Love, Haunted by Loss

Travis, Marion. "An Introduction to the Story of the Cameron Ghost." *Waco Heritage & History*, Fall 1979.

West, Tommy. "The Story of the Cameron House Ghost." *Waco Tribune-Herald*, June 25, 1966.

Towering Above the Brazos Once Again: Restoring Baylor's Old Main Towers

Hunt, Eleanor L. "Towers Going Back atop Baylor's Old Main, Burleson Hall." *Waco Heritage & History*, Summer 1975.

Waco Tribune-Herald. "Reconstructed Towers Link Past, Present at BU." June 19, 1975.

The Stories We Tell: The (So Far) Missed Opportunity of the Taylor Museum

Ament, Jill. "Local Historians Correct Marker Mistaking Important Tribal History." KWBU.org.

Hillen, Michelle. "Waco Museum's Founder Pushing to Reopen Doors for Public Tours." *Houston Chronicle*, September 8, 2002.

Ruiz, Kyle. "Helen Marie Taylor Museum of Waco History." wacohistory.org.

Waco Citizen. "Historic Day in Waco: Ground Broken for the Helen Marie Taylor Museum." July 17, 1990.

About the Author

Eric S. Ames is assistant director for marketing and communication for Baylor University's Libraries & ITS and an adjunct professor in Baylor's Department of Museum Studies. In 2019, he was awarded the City of Waco's Historic Landmark Preservation Commission's Excellence in Education Award for his efforts to preserve and promote Waco history. His previous works on Waco history include Images of America: *Waco* and Images of Modern America: *Waco* by Arcadia Publishing. You can find him on Twitter at @EricAmes628.